Henry Fielding
and the Heliodoran Novel

Henry Fielding
and the Heliodoran Novel

Romance, Epic,
and Fielding's New Province
of Writing

James J. Lynch

Rutherford ● Madison ● Teaneck
Fairleigh Dickinson University Press
London and Toronto: Associated University Presses

Associated University Presses
440 Forsgate Drive
Cranbury, NJ 08512

Associated University Presses
25 Sicilian Avenue
London WC1A 2QH, England

Associated University Presses
2133 Royal Windsor Drive
Unit 1
Mississauga, Ontario
Canada L5J 1K5

The paper used in this publication meets the requirements of the American National Standard for Permanence of Paper for Printed Library Materials Z39.48-1984.

Library of Congress Cataloging-in-Publication Data

Lynch, James J., 1951-
　　Henry Fielding and the Heliodoran novel.

　　Bibliography: p.
　　Includes index.
　　1. Fielding, Henry, 1707-1754—Criticism and inter-
pretation. 2. Literary form. 3. Romances—History and
criticism. 4. Epic literature—History and criticism.
I. Title.
PR3457.L96　　1986　　　　823'.5　　　　85-27402
ISBN 0-8386-3268-8

Printed in the United States of America

For my grandfather,
John J. Lynch,
and my wife,
Marilyn Kovac Lynch—
each a source of strength, inspiration, and love.

Contents

Preface

In *The Rise of the Novel* Ian Watt claims that, for any literary genre but the novel, we are concerned with "the author's skill in handling the formal conventions of that genre."[1] Our critical understanding of the novel, he contends, must be different: "since the novelist's primary task is to convey the impression of fidelity to human experience, attention to any preestablished formal conventions can only endanger his success."[2] Such statements make sense only if we presuppose that the eighteenth-century English novel is completely different from the prose fiction that preceded it. Further, they make sense only if we confine ourselves to the influence Defoe and Richardson had on the later prominence the novel gives to realism.

When we consider the novels of Henry Fielding, however, it is clear that Watt's theory is incomplete. Like his contemporaries, Fielding often condemns earlier prose fiction as "romance," implying what that term frequently denotes in the eighteenth century: a long-winded, improbable, shapeless work of mere diversion. Yet despite his condemnation of romance, Fielding does not, as Defoe and Richardson do, completely break away from the literary tradition of romance. Indeed, his novels cannot be appreciated exclusively as products of what Watt calls "formal realism." Fielding sifts reality through a narrator who is conscious both of the archetypal assumptions of romance and of the literary patterns by which those archetypes are made into art. Particularly in his two comic novels, *Joseph Andrews* and *Tom Jones,* Fielding takes the wish-fulfillment dream upon which all romance is founded and finds a novelistic shape for it that is at once innovative and conventional.

This book attempts to show how Fielding's attention to some of the formal conventions of romance actually enriches his novels.

It offers a literary historical context for the romance conventions that Fielding redefines for his "new Province of Writing." I argue that, although he condemns as romance such novels as the *Grand Cyrus,* he shares virtually the same aesthetic assumptions as Mme. de Scudéry and other heroic novelists. Like Fielding, these writers sought to elevate prose fiction to the literary status of the epic. In doing so, they attempted to make realistic what was improbable in earlier romances and to make regular what was lacking in artistic design. I show that the heroic novelists found a precedent for their notion of the prose epic in Heliodorus's postclassical Greek romance, the *Aethiopica.* Indeed, the *Aethiopica*'s structure—a journey of two lovers, culminating in a marriage—became the dominant structure for serious romance. Fielding modifies this structure in each of his major novels.

I call this tradition of seventeenth-century epics in prose the *Heliodoran novel*—a term that suggests a different orientation from that of other labels such as the *heroic novel.* The Heliodoran novel is the first sustained effort in European literary history after the Renaissance to subject prose fiction to literary rules. It is a literary synthesis in which writers sought to combine the unity, verisimilitude, and instruction of the epic with the diversity, the marvelous, and the delight of romance. By the mid-seventeenth century, the Heliodoran novel's synthetic nature led prose fiction to become highly rule conscious—so much so that the conventions intended to elevate romance to the status of the epic came to embody for later generations the very essence of romance cliché. Nevertheless, by analyzing how romance conventions in these novels serve a clear aesthetic purpose, we can better understand how Fielding reshapes those conventions in *Joseph Andrews, Tom Jones,* and *Amelia.*

I wish to thank several people whose advice, criticism, and encouragement were invaluable. A. A. Parker, formerly of the University of Texas, inspired the project and first opened my eyes to European prose fiction prior to the eighteenth century. Leo Hughes, of the University of Texas, kept me from straying too far afield in my dissertation on a related topic. Leo Braudy, of the University of Southern California, Jim Garrison, of the University of Texas, and Henry Knight Miller, of Princeton University, each offered wise and insightful criticism. Finally, I must thank my wife and colleague, Marilyn Kovac Lynch. Without her keen editorial skills, not to mention her material and emotional support, this book would not exist.

Henry Fielding
and the Heliodoran Novel

1

Romance, Epic, and Fielding's
New Province of Writing

THE Heliodoran novel is a literary hybrid, a refinement of romance that flourished primarily during the first half of the seventeenth century among writers who sought to apply the rules of epic poetry to prose fiction.[1] Its distinctive form derives from Heliodorus's *Aethiopica*—a postclassical Greek romance that was rediscovered in the mid-sixteenth century and quickly became a central focus in discussions of prose fiction by such literary theorists as Amyot, Scaliger, Tasso, and El Pinciano.[2] Writing in an age that commonly regarded romance as formless and improbable—an idle, if not a dangerous, amusement—these critics saw the *Aethiopica* as an ancient precedent for the epic in prose. Its *in medias res* structure provided a form wherein the diversity of episodes characteristic of romance could be unified. Moreover, because its unity of form controlled narrative suspense, the *Aethiopica* achieved a balance between verisimilitude and the marvelous, a combination that allows both instruction and delight.

During the sixteenth century, the *Aethiopica* influenced a variety of novels: in Spain, Núñez's *Clareo y Florisea* (1552) and Montemayor's *Diana* (1559); in England, Greene's *Pandosto* (1558) and Sidney's *Arcadia* (1590); in France, Chappuys's translation of the *Amadís* (1581) and Montreux's *Oeuvre de la Chastété* (1595-99).[3] In the first half of the seventeenth century, the *Aethiopica* became even more widely associated with literary theories about the prose epic. Cervantes, for example, capsulizes the arguments advanced by Tasso, Scaliger, and

El Pinciano in the Canon of Toledo's discourse on romances in *Don Quixote*.[4] Although the Canon does not specifically cite Heliodorus, he does envision an ideal romance that would measure up to the theoretical model of the epic in prose. Cervantes himself puts this ideal into practice in his final novel, *Persiles y Sigismunda* (1617)—a work that, in his phrase, "dares to compete with Heliodorus."[5]

During the first half of the seventeenth century, Heliodorus's novel was widely imitated. It influenced, for example, John Barclay's *Argenis* (1621), a political allegory that anticipates the French heroic novels.[6] By the time Charles Sorel wrote *Le Berger Extravagante* in 1627, Heliodorus was popular enough among literary theorists to rank beside Homer, Vergil, Ariosto, and Tasso in Clarimond's condemnation of all fiction.[7] Racine, it is alleged, memorized the *Aethiopica* when his tutor threatened to take away his copy.[8] Heliodorus's novel even influenced Baltasar Gracián's *El Criticón* (1650-54), a work that combines baroque allegory with the picaresque formula.[9]

Heliodorus's most important influence on prose fiction, however, develops in the heroic novels of Gomberville, La Calprenède, and Scudéry. Scudéry cites Heliodorus as her model in the prefaces to both *Ibrahim* (1641) and the *Grand Cyrus* (1649). By the time Pierre-Daniel Huet wrote his treatise on the novel in 1670, the association of the *Aethiopica* with the prose epic had become so much a part of literary theory that he called Heliodorus the Homer of the novel.

The century-long vogue of the *Aethiopica*—from its first vernacular translation in 1547 to the heroic novels of the mid-seventeenth century—says less about the intrinsic merits of Heliodorus's novel than it does about the desire of theorists and novelists alike to elevate prose fiction to the status of poetry, to give it aesthetic legitimacy. With Heliodorus as a relatively ancient precedent, novelists could effect a synthesis between epic and romance in which diversity could be unified, in which the marvelous could be made verisimilar, and in which instruction could go hand in hand with delight.

The Heliodoran novel by no means accounts for all of the categories of romance that literary historians identify in sixteenth- and seventeenth-century prose fiction, yet it draws from many of them. Like the pastoral novel and the sentimental novel, it emphasizes love and the attendant narrative complications of a love plot: separations, reunions, jealousies, reconciliations. Like the broad category the adventure novel and its subcategory the heroic novel, it emphasizes perilous journeys, military exploits, and conflicts between love and honor. What distinguishes the Heliodoran tradition from other traditions is its very synthetic nature, its consciousness of literary rules.

I shall argue that Henry Fielding's major novels—*Joseph Andrews, Tom Jones,* and *Amelia*—are affected by a synthesis of romance and epic remarkably similar to that in the Heliodoran novel. By the time Fielding founds his "new Province of Writing," the conventions that novelists such as Scudéry had derived from Heliodorus became the very clichés that Fielding and his contemporaries saw as the essence of romance. Yet, instead of abandoning romance altogether in favor of what Ian Watt calls "formal realism," Fielding sought to combine the conventions of romance with the newer conventions of realism. By using the Heliodoran novel as a point of comparison, we can see how Fielding makes serious-romance conventions comic and, indeed, how the very structure of romances such as the Heliodoran novel lies at the core of Fielding's novels.

I do not claim the Heliodoran novel as a hitherto unacknowledged source of Fielding's novels. There is no evidence that Fielding was familiar with the *Aethiopica,* or with Cervantes' *Persiles,* although translations of both were certainly available in the eighteenth century. Fielding refers to some of the French heroic novels that I would place in the Heliodoran tradition, but the influence these works may have had on his novels is somewhat sketchy.[10] Indeed, the closest link comes secondhand, by means of Paul Scarron's *Roman Comique*— a work that not only burlesques heroic novel conventions but also uses the narrative formula that heroic novelists inherited from the *Aethiopica.*

I do contend, however, that the synthesis between epic and romance in the Heliodoran novel parallels the synthesis between romance and history in Fielding's novels. By examining these parallels, we shall discover not only a literary context for the romance assumptions that underlie his works but also a more specific sense of how Fielding integrates romance into the novel form.[11] In one sense, the Heliodoran novel displaces archetypal patterns that Fielding's novels displace further.[12] Yet because novelists in the Heliodoran tradition sought to elevate romance to the literary status of the epic, romance conventions in their works are rhetorical as well as archetypal. I shall argue that Fielding, like the Heliodoran novelists, is self conscious about the literary rhetoric of romance and sought to elevate it, in his comic epics, to a more artful level. To illustrate this I shall construct a paradigm, a synthetic model of the Heliodoran novel and compare it to Fielding's novels. In this manner we may see both what Fielding accepts from the literary rhetoric of serious romance and what he reshapes for his new province of writing. Thus, through the isolation of romance elements in Fielding's novels, we not only gain insight into the author's connection to the tradition of literary romance before him, but we also learn about the connection between romance and the literary developments of sentimentalism in the novels of the second half of the eighteenth century.

Fielding's Novels and the Heliodoran Form

In the next chapter I shall demonstrate how the critical response to the *Aethiopica* influences the structure of such works as Cervantes' *Persiles y Sigismunda* and Scudéry's *Ibrahim* and *Grand Cyrus*. But for the moment let me briefly describe its typical structure. The Heliodoran novel is essentially an epic of love, in which both hero and heroine receive relatively equal narrative attention. Its usual pattern consists of the journey of two lovers who are betrothed and who assume a disguise (often as brother and sister). They travel to a destination where their identities can be revealed and their betrothal vows completed. During the journey they are subjected to many of the accidents one expects of adventure fiction: separations, pursuits by rivals, abductions, supposed deaths, miraculous resurrections, rumored infidelities, tender reunions and reconciliations. At the end of the journey the lovers undergo a final test, the result of which is the unveiling of their identities and their marriage. In addition, the Helidoran novel reflects many of the rhetorical devices common to the epic: *in medias res* openers, lengthy recitals of offstage or antecedent action, stylized descriptions of battles or characters, rhetorical complaints about fortune, and heroic similes and analogies.

Each of Fielding's novels reflects this narrative pattern to a greater or lesser degree. The love story of Joseph Andrews and Fanny, for instance, is an almost naive version of it. It consists of a journey in which the hero and heroine first seek one another (during which quest the hero is robbed and stripped naked and the heroine is nearly raped); then the couple travel back to Lady Booby's country estate, where they expect to be married. At the destination, their marriage is prevented by Lady Booby's jealousy and later by a partial revelation of identity that makes Joseph and Fanny, like the hero and heroine of the Heliodoran novel, appear to be brother and sister. Eventually, a complete unveiling of their identities elevates them in status and allows their marriage. In *Jonathan Wild, Tom Jones,* and *Amelia* the pattern operates less naively, but many of the romance elements in these novels parallel conventions of the Heliodoran novel: the separation of lovers and the assaults on heroines in all three works; the revelation of Tom Jones's identity; and the restoration of the Booths' and the Heartfrees' fortune in the endings of *Amelia* and *Jonathan Wild* respectively.

The romance conventions that emerge in *Joseph Andrews, Tom Jones,* and *Amelia* imply a kind of narrative control that serves to qualify the pose Fielding adopts as a historian. Indeed, in these three works, the more Fielding shifts toward representational realism, the more the romance elements, although still conventional, are displaced in the direction of eighteenth-century sentimentalism. In *Joseph Andrews* the marriage of the lovers occurs after a set of purely conventional complications. In *Tom Jones* the complications that separate Tom from Sophia are in some respects conventional: parental objections, a journey of the lovers, a mystery of identity that is finally solved after a final, seemingly insurmountable set of obstacles. Yet the allegiance that Fielding's narrator professes to historical truth makes it appear equally possible that the novel could end unhappily as well as happily. The reconciliation of hero and heroine, after Tom's parentage is cleared up and Squire Western's objections are removed, is sentimental— a desire on Sophia's part to see evidence of Tom's goodness of heart. In *Amelia,* although some of its matter is blatantly romanesque in nature (like the hero's and heroine's elopement and the snares laid for their seduction), the portrait Fielding paints of societal vice and corruption, of Booth's waywardness and guilt, of Amelia's constancy and almost excessive wifely forgiveness all make the novel even more sentimental than romance. In *Amelia* the journey that takes place is figurative rather than actual; indeed, although the lovers plan to disguise themselves after their elopement, the masking that takes place is the very hypocrisy of the corrupt world in which Booth participates.

Epic and Romance

Because the Heliodoran novel is quite consciously a synthesis of epic and romance, the comparisons I shall make necessarily raise questions about Fielding's notion of these two terms. *Romance* in the eighteenth century is used both as a semantic equivalent of *novel* and as a term referring to prose fiction that does not measure up to eighteenth-century standards for realism. Clara Reeve's distinction between the two is representative: "The Novel is a picture of real life and manners, and of the times in which it is written. The Romance, in lofty and elevated language, describes what never happened nor is likely to happen."[13] I shall use *romance* to describe those narrative conventions that are guided by a wish-fulfilling world in which poetic justice prevails. I shall use *novel* as a neutral label, referring simply to any long work of prose fiction, regardless of that work's allegiance to realism. *Romance* thus implies a particular disposition of a writer toward the reality he is depicting: one that is guided, to use Henry Knight Miller's phrase, "by a world of symbolic and ceremonial 'reality,' rather than of material and historical 'actuality.' "[14]

The term *epic* poses a different set of problems. Inevitably, it denotes for Fielding and for the theorists and writers of the Heliodoran novel the literary tradition of the classical verse epic. I contend, however, that Fielding and the Heliodoran novelists use the term qualitatively rather than generically. When the Canon of Toledo, for example, says that "Epicks may as well be writ in Prose as in Verse," the context of his remarks suggests something of the literary respectability of the epic—that prose fiction can, like poetry, achieve the "best end of Writing, which is at once to delight and instruct."[15]

The Canon uses *Epick*, I submit, to establish an analogy between the ideal romance and the kind of epic poetry we associate with Homer and Vergil. What is at issue in the analogy, however, is not the specific form of the classical epic, but the potential of writers to create works that would be as much admired among the learned and judicious as the *Iliad*, the *Odyssey*, or the *Aeneid*. Indeed, the Curate's response to the Canon's discourse supports this interpretation. He notes that the chivalric romancers are more to be condemned, because in failing to strive for the kind of ideal the Canon describes, they have "no Regard to good Sense, Art, or Rules; by the Observance of which they might have made themselves as famous in Prose, as the two Princes of the Greek and Latin Poetry are in Verse."[16]

The rules referred to here are aesthetic principles, not generic precepts; that is, they bespeak an author's consciousness of design, his ability to evoke the kind of artistic response among judicious readers that will at once delight and instruct. For the Canon and for Fielding later, these rules can be boiled down to two: verisimilitude and unity. The ideal romance, the Canon suggests, should be as close as possible to truth, yet in discussing this quality he is careful to point out that the writers should strike a balance between make-believe and probability. "Falsehood," he notes, "is so much the more commendable, by how much it more resembles Truth, and is the more pleasing the more it is doubtful and possible."[17] A consciousness of design similarly affects the unity of the novels—the liaison between beginning and middle, middle and end: "Fabulous Tales ought to be suited to the Reader's Understanding, being so contriv'd that all

Impossibilities ceasing, all great Accidents appearing easie, and the Mind wholly hanging in suspence, they may at once surprize, astonish, please, and divert; so that Pleasure and Admiration go Hand in Hand."[18]

Throughout his novels Fielding's pronouncements about the comic epic in prose reflect a high degree of rule consciousness. In the preface to *Joseph Andrews* he equates "comic Romance" with "comic Epic-Poem in Prose."[19] He uses *epic* not as a generic label, but as a descriptive term implying a literary enterprise like tragedy, which can be defined in terms of its constituent parts: action, characters, sentiments, and diction. Works "commonly called Romances," such as the *Grand Cyrus* and others, should not be confused with the epic in prose, Fielding suggests, because they "contain very little Instruction or Entertainment" (*Joseph Andrews,* 4).[20] In this sense *epic* marks the difference between idle romances and the kind Fielding sought to create. Importantly, Fielding does not utterly reject romance. Rather, his purpose is to distinguish "comic Romance" from "serious Romance." Similarly, in the prefatory chapter to book 9 of *Tom Jones* he notes that he would have been content with the label *Romance* (instead of *History*), were it not for the "universal Contempt" it has earned (*Tom Jones,* 489). Writers of novels and romances (i.e., "historical Writers who do not draw their Materials from Records") need only possess paper, pens, ink, and the "manual Capacity of using them." They lack the genius, learning, and knowledge of human nature requisite for those who can "invent good Stories and tell them well" (*Tom Jones,* 488).

Like the Canon, Fielding stresses the importance of truth and unity, while at the same time indicating a consciousness about the rhetorical design of these two qualities. In the prefatory chapter to book 3 of *Joseph Andrews,* for example, Fielding argues that his aim is to depict "not Men, but Manners; not an individual but a Species" (*Joseph Andrews,* 189). He does not merely fantasize, as do "modern Novel and *Atlantis* Writers," whose own "Brains" produce the "Chaos whence all their Materials are collected" (*Joseph Andrews,* 187), nor does he claim to be writing the kind of history whose primary aim is a narrative of chronological or geographical facts. Rather, his history, like *Don Quixote,* is a "History of the World in general"— one polished by "Laws, Arts, and Sciences," which remains as true to human nature today as it was when it was first composed (*Joseph Andrews,* 188).

Fielding's notion of unity, like the Canon's, is closely connected with the rhetorical effect produced by his allegiance to truth. In the prefatory chapter to book 10 of *Tom Jones,* for instance, he warns critics not to condemn hastily any incident in his history as "impertinent and foreign" to his main design merely because the critics do not "immediately conceive in what Manner such Incident may conduce to that Design" (*Tom Jones*, 524). Even when he tells the critic in the prefatory essay to book 17 that he will not intervene on Tom's behalf lest he violate the truth and dignity of history, it is clear that some other power, greater than the hero's own ability to save himself, controls the design of the novel. The very fact that *Tom Jones* must be read twice (or be carefully recollected) before we can appreciate its plot indicates that the kind of history Fielding presents conforms to a preconceived design.

Fielding's fullest statement of the unity that operates in his novels appears in the opening chapter to *Amelia*—a novel that, significantly enough, the author himself associates with the Vergilian and Homeric tradition of epics:

> Life may as properly be called an Art as any other; and the great Incidents in it are no more to be considered as mere Accidents than the several Members of a fine Statue or a noble Poem. The Critics in all these are not content with seeing any Thing to be great, without knowing why and how it came to be so. By examining carefully the several Gradations which conduce to bring every Model to Perfection, we learn truly to know that Science in which the Model is formed: As Histories of this Kind, therefore, may properly be called Models of HUMAN LIFE; so by observing minutely the several Incidents which tend to the Catastrophe or Completion of the whole, and the minute Causes whence those Incidents are produced, we shall best be instructed in this most useful of all Arts, which I call the ART of LIFE. (*Amelia*, 17)[21]

That the history of a life should tend toward a catastrophe or a completion implies a distinctly literary notion of design. The minute causes may entail a horizontal method of narration—one that has what the Canon describes as the "loose Method" of romance. Such a design invites the reader to witness events in a chronological sequence without an initial sense of where those events lead. Yet the design itself implies a vertical perspective: one that is shaped and ordered by a creator aware of literary unity. Like the Heliodoran novelists, Fielding finds a way of reconciling the looseness of romance with a design that has the same rule-conscious spirit of the epic, even though his novels differ in structure from the epic.

2

The Heliodoran Novel

In order to define the Heliodoran tradition and its influence on seventeenth-century prose fiction, I shall focus primarily on three critics—Jacques Amyot, Pierre Daniel Huet, and Georges de Scudéry, and on four novels—the *Aethiopica,* the *Persiles,* the *Ibrahim,* and the *Grand Cyrus.* Amyot's preface to the first vernacular translation of the *Aethiopica* (1547) sets the pattern for later sixteenth-century critical reactions to Heliodorus's novel. Huet's *Traité sur l'origine des romans* (1670), written after the heroic-novel vogue had passed, defines the kind of aesthetic regularity that Heliodorus's novel had brought to the mid-seventeenth century French novel. Georges de Scudéry's preface to his sister's *Ibrahim* (1641) discusses the rules of the epic in prose that are evident in both Amyot's preface and in Huet's treatise and, in addition, follows the same kind of Aristotelian schema that Fielding uses in the preface to *Joseph Andrews.*

These three critics capsulize the theoretical foundation of the Heliodoran novel. From the four novels I have generated a paradigmatic model of the Heliodoran novel, defining its characteristics in terms of Aristotle's discussion of tragic poetry: action, character, thought, diction. The *Aethiopica,* of course, establishes the pattern that Cervantes' *Persiles* and Scudéry's *Ibrahim* and *Grand Cyrus* transform into conventions. From this discussion I shall be able to define the rhetorical function of these conventions and see how they are integrated into a coherent whole.

Amyot

Amyot begins his preface with the concession one should expect of a critic writing in an age that regarded prose fiction as idle, if not dangerous. Just as nurses should not "indifferently recite all sorts of fables to small infants lest their minds, from the beginning, be steeped in folly," so, he reasons, one might advise persons who have arrived at the age of reason "not to amuse themselves injudiciously by reading all sorts of fabulous books, lest their understanding slowly accustom itself to love lies and to feed on vanity."[1] He argues, however, that the weakness of our nature makes it necessary for us to divert ourselves occasionally from serious study so that we might better accomplish important things. Noting that a good understanding delights most in seeing, hearing, and understanding something new, Amyot settles on history as the most desirable form of diversion, yet he adds an important series of qualifications to this choice. Since history must relate things as they *have* happened, and not as we might wish them to happen, it is a bit too severe for readers seeking diversion. A historian cannot fill in the gaps of truth by fabulous inventions or too embellished a style lest he detract from his principal aim, namely, "to instruct by examples from the past about affairs of the future."[2] What is needed, Amyot implies, is a kind of disguised history whose primary aim is to divert, but to divert in a studied, artful manner: "Just as in painting those tableaus are judged to be better and more pleasing to the eyes which better represent nature, so in [disguised histories] those which are less removed from nature and where there is more verisimilitude are more pleasing to those who measure truth by reason and who delight by studied judgment."[3]

To define his notion of disguised histories, Amyot comments on two authorities. The first is Horace, who teaches that dissembled things, in order to delight, must approach truth; from this precept Amyot reasons that "it is not necessary that everything be feigned, for that is not permitted for poets themselves."[4] Next, Amyot cites Strabo's *Geography,* commenting on that author's formula for poetic invention, which consists of three things:

> First, in history, whose aim is truth: for this reason it is not lawful for poets, when they write of things in nature, to write at their pleasure other than what is true, for that would be imputed not to license or artifice, but to ignorance. Second, in order and disposition, the aim of which is the expression and power of attracting and engaging the reader. Third, in the fiction, whose aims are the astonishment and the delight that proceed from the novelty of things strange and filled with marvel.[5]

From these three principles—truth, order, and fiction—Amyot formulates a statement about the ideal disguised history that anticipates the Canon of Toledo's discourse on romance: "One should not permit all things in fiction that he wishes to disguise under the name of historical truth; rather, he ought to interlace truth closely with falsehood, always dexterously retaining the semblance of truth, and to join the whole so that there is no discordance from the beginning to the middle, nor from the middle to the end."[6]

Like the Canon of Toledo, Amyot sees the romances of the previous age as unprofitable if not dangerous, because they teach the unlearned to love falsehood. Lacking erudition, knowledge of antiquity, or anything from which one might be instructed, earlier romances are

> so badly sewn together and so far from all the appearance of verisimilitude that they seem rather the dreams of a sick man tossing in a hot fever than the inventions of a man of genius and judgment. And, therefore, in my opinion, they have neither the grace nor the power of delighting a good mind, for they are not worthy of it. And it is a certain sign that there is nothing ingenious and noble which delights the stupid and the common.[7]

The *Aethiopica* offers the proper balance of truth, order, and fiction, in Amyot's view. Its discourses, taken from natural and moral philosophy, offer the erudition he finds lacking in more recent romances. Its story portrays human passion "with so great honesty that one cannot find an example in it of evil doing;"[8] immoral and dishonest affections in Heliodorus's novel lead to unhappiness, while moral and honest ones lead to happiness. Above all, Heliodorus measures up to the standards of unity thought most desirable among Renaissance neoclassicists:

> He begins in the middle of the history, as do heroic poets, which causes, *prima facie,* a great astonishment among readers and engenders in them an impassioned desire to understand the beginning and yet still draws the reader into the story by an ingenious liaison, so that one is not certain about everything he finds in the beginning of the first book until he has read the end of the fifth. And when he arrives there, he has a great longing to see the end, whereas before he longed to see the beginning. Thus, one's understanding remains suspended until he arrives at the conclusion, which leaves the reader satisfied, as those people are satisfied who come to an ardently desired and long-awaited joy.[9]

The *in medias res* beginning, of course, allies Heliodorus with the epic poets—a connection consistently noted by later critics—but beyond the respectability epic brings to prose fiction, Amyot is more concerned with the control such a pattern offers. The beginning puts the reader's mind in immediate suspense, and when the initial mystery is solved, the reader has been made aware of a further mystery that will not be solved until the very end of the novel. This carefully arranged tightening and loosening of complications makes one aware of literary design—of the art, as Fielding phrases it, of inventing stories and telling them well.

Huet

The implicit rules that Amyot finds in the *Aethiopica* are regulations about presenting fiction as truth. In Huet's treatise, written at the end of the Heliodoran-novel vogue, regularity itself is the primary concern. Like Cervantes and Amyot, Huet criticizes earlier romances, particularly romances of chivalry, as lacking artistic design. They are "an accumulation of fictions grossly heaped together one on top of another."[10] The romances of his era are more refined, "regular." They differ from poetry in degree, not in kind:

> Romances are simpler, less lofty, and less figurative in invention and expression. Poems have more of the marvelous, although they sometimes contain the verisimilar. Poems are more regular and more polished in their arrangement, and they have fewer incidents and episodes. Romances have more because they are less lofty and figurative. They do not expand the mind so much but leave it in an altered state by a greater number of ideas. Finally, poems have a military or political action as subject; they deal with love only occasionally. Novels, on the other hand, have love as their principal subject; they deal with politics and war only incidentally.[11]

The *Aethiopica* reflects the qualities that Huet admires in the regular romance. He regards Heliodorus as the founder of epic prose fiction, providing a source from which all who have followed him have drunk, just as poets have drunk from the wellspring of Homer. Like Amyot and other critics, Huet praises the *Aethiopica* for its arrangement and verisimilitude:

> One notices in it much fertility and invention. The incidents are frequent, novel, verisimilar, well-ordered and well-untangled. Its denouement is admirable, natural, born of the subject matter, and nothing is more touching or moving.[12]

Befitting his notion that romances should have love as their principal subject, Huet praises the ability of Heliodorus's formal design to affect the passions. The "horror" of the sacrifice at the end of the novel, in which Theagenes and Chariclea are to be immolated, is followed by the "joy" the reader experiences both in seeing her escape from danger through the recognition of her parents and in seeing the heroine married to the hero.

The rules about prose fiction that emerge from Huet's comparison of romance with poetry and from his discussion of the *Aethiopica* are based on the Aristotelian and Horatian premises widely accepted during the Heliodoran vogue. Romances can be allowed a variety of incidents, but the delight and instruction to be found in that variety result from its skillful arrangement and closeness to truth. This sort of romance, in short, assumes a readership sophisticated enough to discern the art that controls make believe.

Georges de Scudéry

A similar consciousness about the art of prose fiction dominates Georges de Scudéry's preface to *Ibrahim*. "Every art," he states, "hath its certain rules, which by infallible means lead to the ends proposed."[13] The rules he proposes are very similar to those discussed by Cervantes, Amyot, and Huet, but what makes Scudéry's preface distinctive is that he not only defends *Ibrahim* in theoretical terms but he also interprets the theory in light of the novel.

He begins his discourse by noting that his precedents are the "famous Romanzes of Antiquity" that have imitated the epic poem. Like Huet's, Scudéry's principal model is the *Aethiopica*—a work that he utters in the same breath as the *Iliad,* the *Odyssey,* the *Aeneid,* and *Jerusalem Delivered.* With these ancient romances as precedents, he defines the features of the *Ibrahim* in terms of Aristotle's divisions: action, character, thought, and style.

The rules for action consist of the same three principles that concerned other theorists attracted to Heliodorus and the epic tradition: unity, verisimilitude, and well-ordering. Unity results from the "principal action whereunto all the rest, which reign over all the work are fastned, and which makes them that they are not employed, but for the conducting of it to its perfection" (Scudéry, 2). Like Cervantes, Scudéry values diversity in unity. Just as the epic poem has diverse episodes, so the epic in prose has diverse "histories." The rule of unity, however, provides a framework or a central narrative path from which those episodes or histories can diverge.

Well-ordering means both the *in medias res* opener that many earlier critics admired in the *Aethiopica* and what critics of drama called the "unity of time." Beginning in the middle for Scudéry (as for Amyot) creates suspense and provides a framework within which the principal action can be confined to a reasonable boundary of time: one year. Other narrative details can be delivered by recitals, thus further allowing diversity within the unity.

Even more than the other two qualities, however, Scudéry places the most emphasis on verisimilitude. It is the foundation on which the work is built: "without it nothing can move, without it nothing can please" (Scudéry, 4). It is a "charming deceiver" which, if not present, would make the work disgusting. Verisimilitude results from studying the "Manners, Customs, Religions, and Inclinations of People," and from drawing characters from illustrious persons of history. By attending to both, Scudéry argues, an author can achieve instruction and delight:

> for whenas falshood and truth are confounded by a dexterous hand, wit hath much adoe to disintangle them, and is not easily carried to destroy that which pleaseth it; contrarily, whenas invention doth not make use of this artifice, and that falshood is produced openly, this gross untruth makes no impression in the soul, nor gives any delight. (Scudéry, 4)

To create verisimilitude the author should have a conscious control over the variety of incidents. Scudéry notes that the more "natural" the adventures are, the more satisfaction they give: "the ordinary course of the Sun seems more marvellous to me, than the strange and deadly rayes of Comets; for which reason it is also that I have not caused so many Shipwrecks, as there are in some ancient Romanzes" (Scudéry, 5). Just as Huet has a sliding scale to determine the difference between the amount of diversity appropriate to romance and to poetry, so Scudéry accepts a sliding scale about the "natural" quantity of marvelous incidents such as shipwrecks. He does not entirely banish shipwrecks; he simply urges their use in moderation.

Scudéry's comments on character reflect a similar concern with moderation as a means of achieving verisimilitude. A hero should not be "oppressed with such a prodigious quantity of accidents," as has been the usual practice among earlier romancers because the character then would be "far from true resemblance, the life of no man having been so cross'd" (Scudéry, 5). He advocates, instead, that the author spread such accidents among diverse characters so that their histories still appear "both fertile and judicious together" and still within the bounds of "this so necessary true resemblance" (Scudéry, 6).

By a similar reasoning, he argues that in order to represent "true heroical courage" the hero should accomplish something extraordinary, but that he should not "continue in that sort" lest those "incredible actions . . . degenerate into ridiculous Fables, and never move the mind" (Scudéry, 6). He argues further that a hero should not display a "brutish valour" but should possess enough virtue of character to understand the events in which he participates. By thinking valorous thoughts the hero will display a nobility of character that Scudéry later notes need not necessarily be confined to kings and princes. Like Theagenes and Chariclea in the *Aethiopica,* Justinian and Isabelle in the *Ibrahim* are not royal, but they possess sufficient qualities to rule over the whole world.

The valorous thoughts of verisimilar characters, according to Scudéry, conform to a sense of decorum that is a dominant characteristic of the French heroic novels.[14] This sense of decorum is even more pronounced in Scudéry's discussion of thought or theme. In the spirit of neoclassical moralism Scudéry remarks that virtue is always rewarded and vice punished in *Ibrahim.* The faults of "great ones" (such as Soliman, presumably, who is the principal cause of distress for the hero and heroine) result from love and ambition: the "noblest of passions" (Scudéry, 8). Yet, for reasons of decorum the hero is not subjected to amorous temptations, as other romance heroes are, because it would "clash with Civility in the person of Ladies, and of true resemblance in that of men" (Scudéry, 8). Men, he notes, are rarely cruel to ladies and could not be so "with any good grace."

Scudéry's sense of decorum suggests that the charming deceit in verisimilitude reflects the life and customs of the *salons.* Indeed, this sense of decorum is particularly evident in his remarks on style. He argues that a narrative style should not be more "inflated" than that of ordinary conversation: "the more facile it is, the more excellent it is . . . the less constraint it hath, the more perfection it hath" (Scudéry, 13). *Ibrahim* aims, he suggests, at a "just mediocrity between vicious Elevation and creeping lowness."

Structure of the Heliodoran Novel

It must certainly be difficult for novel-oriented readers to understand why seventeenth-century writers were fascinated with Heliodorus. The *Aethiopica* unfolds like a series of Chinese boxes— hardly a model for anything but the most contrived unity and realism. Similarly, a novel-oriented reader might scoff at Scudéry's quantitative notion of verisimilitude, which includes some shipwrecks, but not too many, and some fabulous adventures, but not too many for a single character. Indeed, if a novel-oriented reader had the patience to struggle through the myriad of adventures the hero undergoes in the 6,000-or-so pages of the *Grand Cyrus,* that reader might wonder just what sense of unity Scudéry intended about heroic action.

Fiction's resemblance to truth, however, is always a slippery matter, subject to conventions guided by different artistic assumptions. Is a photo-realistic painting, for example, any more "real" than a mannerist painting? The texture and composition of the former are manipulated so that it appears not to be painting at all, and the distortion of perspective in the latter makes some limbs appear larger than life. Yet the former is a painting, not a photograph, and the images in the latter still create the impression of real human figures.

Writers of the works that emerge in the Heliodoran tradition are more content with a stylized representation of truth than writers in the later tradition of the novel. Indeed, one reason why works such as the *Grand Cyrus* passed out of vogue is that they were too stylized, too conventional. They become too much a part of the literary Establishment: long-winded, corpulent, clichéd. Nevertheless, the impulse to stylize gives the Heliodoran novel its distinctive form.

What distinguishes the Heliodoran novel from the general pool of romance is that writers in this tradition are conscious of following the precedents of Heliodorus's epic in prose, and, in so doing, they also adapt the narrative pattern of the *Aethiopica.* Indeed, the narrative pattern defines the particular rhetorical values of the romance conventions in it. To analyze the pattern, I have compared elements in the *Aethiopica* with Cervantes' imitation of that work, *Persiles y Sigismunda* (1617), and with Scudéry's *Ibrahim* (1641) and *Grand Cyrus* (1649). Elements of the pattern I describe can also be found in other heroic novels, such as Gomberville's *Polexandre* (1637) and La Calprenède's *Cassandre* (1642), as well as in works not related to the heroic-novel tradition, such as Barclay's *Argenis* (1621) and Gracián's *El Criticón* (1650-54). All of these novels are richly textured, with intrinsic merits that my formulaic approach here cannot do justice to. Nevertheless, reducing these works to a common denominator provides a way of understanding how they synthesize conventions of romance into a form that has the unity, diversity, verisimilitude, and the marvelous that are essential for the epic in prose.

Typically, the Heliodoran novel presents the story of two lovers who are betrothed, yet whose marriage is impeded by parental objection. The lovers are both of noble birth, yet for one reason or another they are forced to conceal their identities. In disguise, often as brother and sister, they embark on a journey toward a place where their identities can be revealed and where they can be married. On the journey they are separated and reunited several times and beset with many of the adventures usually associated with romance literature: shipwrecks, abductions, pursuits by rival lovers, lengthy recitals of offstage heroics, supposed deaths, miraculous resurrections, supposed infidelity, impassioned jealousy, tender reconciliations. When they arrive at their destination, the lovers undergo a penultimate medley of complications that seem to make their ultimate happiness impossible. Eventually, however, the hand of providence wins out; the hero and heroine reveal their true identities, the obstacles to their marriage are removed, and the couple weds. Although the Heliodoran novel characteristically thrusts the reader *in medias res,* its action, straightened out chronologically, consists of four phases: (1) the love of hero and heroine; (2) the journey; (3) the arrival at the destination and the penultimate complications; (4) the marriage.

In each of these phases, elements of action and character are closely interrelated. In the first phase, the love of hero and heroine develops in secrecy. Usually the real identity of one or the other protagonist is mysterious, a fact that must be resolved by the end of the novel. Often either the hero or heroine has resolved never to fall in love, and, as a result, the love is first revealed as a love malady—a conventional circumstance in much romance literature. Often the hero is an outsider, and the heroine's father or guardian has another suitor in mind for his charge. This parental impediment becomes a continuing source of conflict that the hero and heroine must eventually resolve. Typically, in this phase, however, they simply decide to avoid it by launching on a journey. In some of the Heliodoran novels there is a ritual of betrothal, in which the hero and heroine exchange vows and agree to disguise themselves, often as brother and sister. In many of the Heliodoran novels the lovers are aided by some friendly companion who assumes the roles of intermediary, confidant, and surrogate parent.

Phase two—the journey—usually takes up the bulk of the narrative. The lovers are typically separated and reunited several times, thus testing their fidelity to one another and their faith in the guiding hand of providence. During the separations, one or the other lover might be presumed unfaithful or even thought dead; the lovers' reunion later on quiets the jealousy or despair that these false rumors propagate. Both the hero and heroine are subject to the amorous advances of other characters in this phase, but usually the hero has more rivals than the heroine—and these might range from the purely villainous to the noble. In addition to rivals, this phase also introduces such other characters as sympathetic companions, who themselves usually have stories that swell the narrative and reflect, thematically, on the story of the hero and heroine.

In phase three the hero and heroine arrive at their destination and typically suffer through a final series of complications before their identities can be revealed. Although the sources of conflict vary, all the Heliodoran novelists present a convergence of narrative complications that make the marriage of hero and heroine seem impossible. Finally, however, the mystery surrounding either the hero's or the heroine's identity is cleared up, usually through the agency of some other character, who appears on the scene because of accident or divine providence. With the hero and heroine's identities revealed and unmasked, they marry. Phase four is typically nothing more than a ritualistic celebration of an impending happy-ever-after.

Phase One: The Love of Hero and Heroine

The first phase is characteristically reported as antecedent action. In the *Aethiopica,* for instance, books 2 through 5 consist largely of Calasiris's account of how Chariclea and Theagenes fall in love. Chariclea, the assumed daughter of Caricles, ruler of Delphos, scorns any suitors that her father proposes but nevertheless falls in love with Theagenes, who comes to Delphos as an Athenian representative in the sacrifice at the altars of Apollo. He is a descendant of Achilles and, as such, adumbrates that hero in his appearance:

> Therewith entered a young man of Achilles courage in deede, who in countenance, and stomacke appeared no lesse, with a streight necke, hie foreheaded with his haire in comely sorte rebending downe, his nosthrilles wide inough to take breathe, which is a token of courage and strength: his eyes not very grey, but grey and blacke, which made him looke somewhat fiercely, and yet not very aimiably, not much unlike the Sea, which is calmed after a boysterous tempest.[15]

After Theagenes wins the traditional games at Delphos, Chariclea is smitten with a malady that Calasiris (the couple's guide and surrogate father) is enjoined to cure. Calasiris discovers that the cause of the malady is her love for Theagenes and also learns, by the inscriptions on a ribbon that she possesses, that she is actually the daughter of the king and queen of Ethiopia, who abandoned her as an infant. In the meantime, Chariclea's adoptive father plans to marry her to a kinsman, Alcamenes. Calasiris then becomes an intermediary between the two lovers and arranges for them to escape from Delphos.

Since the novel begins in the middle of things, by the time we learn of the hero and heroine's love we have already been smitten by the beauty and the noble deportment of the heroine. Chariclea is described in the first book as "a maid endued with excellent beautie, which might be supposed a goddesse." Indeed, Chariclea adumbrates Diana: "She had a garland of laurell on her head, a quiver on her backe, and in her lefte hand a bowe, leaning upon her thigh with the other hand" (*Aethiopica*, 10). We later learn from Calasiris's account that Theagenes is under the special protection of Diana's brother, Apollo. The love of the hero and heroine is thus complementary on a symbolic level; their earthly plan to disguise themselves as brother and sister, until such time as Chariclea can secure her inheritance, is divinely sanctioned. With Calasiris—a priest, a father figure, and an intermediator—the lovers seem guided by providence.

Similarly, albeit in a less ritualized manner, the initial phase of the *Persiles,* the *Ibrahim,* and the *Cyrus* presents a love conflict that necessitates a journey and involves some problem of identity. In the *Persiles* the information about the hero and heroine's falling in love is not reported until the third last chapter of the novel, a narrative decision that stretches the *in medias res* structure to its limit. There we learn that the hero, Periandro, is actually Persiles, the second son of Queen Eustoquia of Thule. He met Sigismunda (who assumes the name Auristela during the journey) when she was sent to Thule by her mother, the queen of Friesland, in order marry Persiles' older brother. During the visit, the hero falls in love with her and suffers a love malady. Eventually his mother intervenes and arranges for the hero and heroine, disguised as brother and sister, to venture to Rome, where the heroine can be instructed in the true faith.

In the *Ibrahim* and the *Cyrus* the initial phase is told immediately after the dramatic opening of the novels. Justinian, who is forced to assume the name Ibrahim when he is captured by Sultan Soliman of Constantinople, fell in love with the heroine, Isabelle Grimaldi of Genoa, because of her exquisite beauty. They exchanged letters in secret because of her father's objection, but this parental objection is removed after Justinian defends the heroine's father from political enemies. The couple are to be wed and to inherit Monaco; however, their marriage is prevented when Justinian is banished from Genoa by the rival political faction. Although the pair do not immediately embark on a journey, such an event occurs later in the novel when Justinian is reunited with Isabelle during his leave of absence from his service as Soliman's illustrious Bassa.

In the *Cyrus,* the initial phase depends upon the hero's disguising himself as Artamène because an oracle at his birth proclaimed that he would conquer all of Asia. This prediction causes his maternal grandfather to worry about the future of his own kingdom and that of his son, King Cyaxare of Cappadocia. Eventually, Artamène enters Cyaxare's court and falls in love with his daughter, Mandane. Although she falls in love with him because of his feats of glory on her father's behalf, when he reveals his real identity, she imposes upon him the mandate that he must find some way of resurrecting Cyrus before she will consent to marry him. This indeed becomes his quest, and leads to the various separations, reunions, and complications of the rest of the novel.

Phase Two: The Journey of the Lovers

The second phase comprises the present action of the Heliodoran novel: the journey into whose middle we are thrust when the novel opens. In the *Aethiopica* this begins with the hero's and heroine's shipwreck at the mouth of the Nile, at which point Chariclea supposes that Theagenes is dead. The lovers are imprisoned by a band of pirates led by Thyamis, who falls in love with the heroine; Thyamis, we later learn, is an exiled priest of Memphis and the son of Calasiris, the couple's guide, intermediary, and father-figure. There is a battle, during which the heroine, this time, is presumed dead. The hero and heroine attempt to escape, but eventually they are separated— Chariclea to rejoin Calasiris, Theagenes to serve as a soldier in Thyamis's army. Eventually the hero and heroine are reunited at Memphis, where Thyamis is restored to his office, where Calasiris dies, and where the hero and heroine are imprisoned by Arsace, the wife of Oroondates (a military champion at war with Ethiopia). Arsace falls in love with the hero and threatens to kill him if he does not submit to her, but eventually her plan backfires and the hero and heroine are delivered into the hands of the king of Ethiopia, Chariclea's father.

In the *Persiles,* the *Cassandre, Ibrahim,* and the *Grand Cyrus,* this second phase encompasses the bulk of the heroic adventures and protracted suspense. In the *Persiles,* more than the other three, the adventures of hero and heroine result from the journey itself. When the novel opens, Periandro and Auristela have both been captured by the pirate-barbarian Corcicurbo. They are immediately separated when Periandro is released and set to sea; he is rescued by Prince Arnaldo, who had previously fallen in love with Auristela when she was sold as a slave into the hands of his father, the king of Denmark. By disguising himself as a woman, Periandro returns to Corcicurbo's island prison where, aided by a family of Christian barbarians, he rescues Auristela. The rest of the second phase consists of their journey to Rome through the perilous northern seas, through Portugal, Spain, France, and Italy. The hero and heroine are separated several times during the journey and subjected to amorous advances of rivals. Prince Arnaldo, for example, remains more or less a constant companion because Auristela, in order to preserve her virginity, pretends that she will marry him when they reach Rome. Later, when the hero and heroine journey through France, the Duke of Nemours falls in love with Auristela, thus providing two rivals for Periandro.

Periandro himself becomes the cause of jealousy for the heroine when the couple are separated early in the journey. In his search for Auristela, Periandro arrives at the island of King Policarpo, whose daughter, Synforoza, falls in love with the hero. Auristela hears rumors of their love from a ship's captain and is dutifully jealous. Unlike the loves of Arnaldo and Nemours, this complication is resolved when the hero and heroine are reunited on Policarpo's island and when, after much ado, they escape from Synforoza and her equally treacherous father.

When the hero and heroine are reunited, the complications that produce suspense largely consist of their efforts to maintain their disguised identities and resist the threats of rivals. The heroine manages to keep suitors at a distance by a combination of duplicity and delay. Auristela, for instance, as has been mentioned, appears to consent to Prince Arnaldo's plan to marry her but tells him that he must wait until they arrive at Rome. In the *Aethiopica,* Chariclea makes a similar arrangement with Thyamis; she pretends to consent to marry him but asks him to wait until they reach Memphis. These complications produce brief moments of despair that intensify narrative suspense. Since we know the hero and heroine are lovers, not brother and sister, the threats of rival lovers momentarily cause us to question the design of providence. The lovers' ability to avert the catastrophe reminds us that providence guides the course of chaste lovers, rough-hewn as that course may be.

In the separation of the lovers, during which considerable narrative energy is expended, we become aware of a successively tightening and loosening knot of complication, the unity-in-diversity that Renaissance critics found in the *Aethiopica.* During the separations, both lovers typically participate in marvelous adventures, which they recount at great length upon their reunion. The heroine is conventionally abducted by pirates, ransomed into seemingly safer hands, and then amorously pursued by her supposed protector. The hero is usually thrust into heroic battles, often as the champion of his rival. Theagenes, for example, eventually becomes Thyamis's champion in the battle of Memphis, even though Thyamis had designs on Chariclea. Ibrahim becomes the champion of Soliman, and Artamène the champion of Cyaxare, even though these rulers stand in the way of their marriage to the heroines. There are endless possible variations on this theme, but however it happens, the hero is inevitably distracted from his pursuit of the heroine because of the narrative necessity of being a hero.

Although military adventures take over much of the French heroic novels, these works nevertheless exploit many of the melodramatic conventions of the Heliodoran novel. During their separations, for example, either the hero or the heroine hears false reports of the other's death or infidelity. In the *Cyrus* Mandane hears that the hero has been fatally wounded in defense of her father (Cyrus's mortal enemy). Later she learns that Cyrus has fallen in love with Princess Araminte. In the *Ibrahim,* after his initial separation from Isabelle, Justinian receives a letter informing him that his beloved has married Prince Masseran.

The supposed death inevitably provokes a lengthy rhetorical complaint against fortune. In book 2 of the *Aethiopica,* for instance, after he supposes that Chariclea is dead, Theagenes, beating his head and tearing his hair, proclaims his despair:

> Farewell this day my life, let here all feare, daungers, cares, hope, and love, have end and be dissolved, Cariclia is dead, Theagenes is destroyed, in vaine was I unhappie man afraide, and content to betake my selfe to flight, which no man would have done, reserving my selfe to thee my sweete heart. Surely my joy, I will live no longer sith thou art dead, not according to the common course of nature, which is a very greevous thing; and has contrary to thine opinion, and not in his protection who was thy whole desire, yealded up thy life. With fire art thou consumed? and in steade of lights at thy marriage, hath God ordeined such lights for thee? The bravest beauty in the world is lost, so that no token of such singular fairnesse remayneth in the dead bodie. (*Aethiopica,* 45-46)

The rhetorical effect of complaints such as these is to heighten immediate suspense; the reader assumes, as does Theagenes, that Chariclea is dead and participates in the hero's melodramatic grief. Moreover, Theagenes is cast in the role of a dutiful mortal, maltreated by the gods. When Chariclea is discovered to be alive, our faith in narrative providence is restored.

When lovers are supposed unfaithful, a similar pattern emerges. The aggrieved complains against fortune and contemplates suicide. Usually, however, the character stoically resolves to submit to whatever accidents fate may produce. After Justinian in the *Ibrahim* learns incorrectly that Isabelle has married, for instance, he resolves, as an alternative to suicide, to seek his fortunes in war. Eventually, he is captured by Soliman's army and faced with death. He thereupon resolves not to oppose his will against fortune. The following passage comes at the end of Justinian's lengthy recital of his adventures since the separation from Isabelle:

> I resolved to receive all that fortune prepared for me, with a design no longer to oppose my reason against her humors, and blandly, and without resistance, to obey this inevitable power, which mocks all human prudence, which puts us into the Port upon the point of shipwracke; which precipitates us from the very top of happiness into the abysme of misery; which overturns thrones, which destroys kingdomes; which causes kings to die; and to say all in a word, which soveraignly disposes of the whole Universe.[16]

A resolve of this sort produces a rhetorical effect similar to that of a hero or heroine's mourning the supposed death of a beloved. Once again we are urged to see the lovers' cruel fortune, but that fortune appears far more cruel when love, in these epics of love, seems to be betrayed. Apparent infidelity, like apparent death, potentially removes the wish-fulfillment from romance.

Phase Three: Arrival at the Destination

In the third phase of the Heliodoran novel, the lovers are brought to their destination and the knots of complication that we expect to be unraveled are tightened further before their final unraveling. In the *Aethiopica,* this phase consists of the trial that Chariclea and Theagenes undergo at Meroe, the capital of Ethiopia and the birthplace of the heroine. Like much of the novel, the further complications and final unraveling take a ritual form: the hero and heroine, having been taken prisoner by the heroine's father, are to be sacrificed at the altars of the sun and the moon. Before their immolation, however, they undergo a trial by fire to verify their purity. After passing this test, Chariclea reveals herself to be the daughter of the king and queen and proves her identity by means of a ribbon and jewels that she has kept in her possession despite all of the adventures she has endured.

The plot seems to be at the edge of a happy resolution, yet Chariclea's father insists that Theagenes be sacrificed, a prospect that naturally brings the heroine to the brink of conventional madness.

Theagenes then performs two heroic feats: he tames a sacrificial bull that runs rampant in the court, and he defeats the hitherto undefeated Ethiopian champion in a wrestling match. Despite these feats, the hero is still to be sacrificed and the heroine to be married to the king's adoptive son. When matters could be no worse, Caricles, the heroine's adoptive father arrives and accuses Theagenes of stealing his daughter. This event provides the final impetus for the plot to be resolved; Theagenes is proved to be of noble birth, and the news of his betrothal to Chariclea is revealed, thus freeing the hero from the threat of sacrifice. The two are then consecrated priest and priestess of the Sun and Moon, appropriate to their Greek protectors, Apollo and Diana. Finally, the two wed.

Three specific conventions capsulize the rapid-fire sequence of events in this phase: (1) the chastity and fidelity of the two lovers is once again tested; (2) a penultimate medley of complications—some old, some new—makes the lovers' marriage seem impossible; (3) some intermediary agent provides information about the hero and heroine that allows them to be married. Because these three elements arise from the unity of the plot, they take on different forms in the novels imitating the *Aethiopica*.

In the *Persiles* Periandro's love is tested by a rich courtesan, Hipólita, who, after an unsuccessful attempt to seduce him, arranges for a witch to inflict Auristela with a beauty-sapping disease. Despite the heroine's ugliness, Periandro remains faithful, unlike the Duke of Nemours, who abandons Auristela when her beauty fades. Even after the heroine recovers, however, the expected ending is further delayed when Auristela decides to dedicate herself to God. This seemingly insurmountable obstacle causes Periandro to leave Rome and, providentially, to meet Seráfido, a traveler from the hero's native land who reveals Periandro's and Auristela's real identities.

In the *Ibrahim* final complications depend less on revelation of identity than on love-honor conflicts. In order for the hero and heroine to marry, Justinian must be freed from his obligation to Soliman—to be freed, in effect, from his forced identity as Ibrahim. In the *Cyrus* the hero's need to disguise himself as Artamène in order to avoid being killed by Mandane's father is removed about two-thirds through the work, but the final resolution can occur only when he has defeated the rival who has plagued him from the beginning. For each of these novels to work out happily, however, there must be a final test of fidelity, a triumph over recent and recurrent obstacles, and an actualization, if not a revelation, of the hero's and heroine's identities.

Phase Four: The Marriage

The fourth phase is the "principal action" to which all the other elements in the plot, according to Georges de Scudéry, are fastened—the marriage of the lovers. Characteristically, authors give the briefest possible attention to this phase. In these epics of love, guided as they are by the narrative analogy of divine providence, marriage is the completion and fulfillment.

Character, Theme, and Style in the Heliodoran Novel

The formula I have sketched focuses on the unity of action that sixteenth- and seventeenth-century admirers of the *Aethiopica* so highly valued. Elements of character, theme, and style differ far more dramatically among the various works in the Heliodoran novel tradition, yet they too follow basic formulae that contribute to the central unity of the plot.

The principal characters in the Heliodoran novel are heroic lovers and, as such, are complementary in nature. Both are of noble birth, although typically they do not enjoy the fullness of their birthrights until they are married. Their nobility, nevertheless, is evident even when they are disguised, because of their remarkable beauty, chastity, and courage. Unlike chivalric novels or traditional verse epics, the Heliodoran novel focuses on the journey of both lovers, not on the peripatetic adventures of a knight serving a lady who remains inactive (the chivalric pattern) or the struggles of a soldier returning from wars to his homeland or to a new land (the pattern of the Homeric and Vergilian epics). The Heliodoran novel celebrates the active wills of both hero and heroine. Both are buffeted by fortune; both are subject to the amorous passions of others. The principal action depends on their mutual happiness.

From the *Aethiopica* onward, the heroine is very often more prominent than the hero. Usually, she is remarkable for her wit and ingenuity, as well as her beauty and chastity. In Heliodorus's novel it is Chariclea who controls Theagenes' fate at the end; indeed, it is she who has fended off suitors throughout the novel. Later Heliodoran heroines maintain their chastity, just as Auristela does, by duplicity and delay. After the model of Chariclea, they display a willfulness that keeps the plot in motion. Auristela, for instance, insists on maintaining her virginity until she and Periandro arrive at Rome, where she can be instructed in the true faith. Even when she is there, as noted above, she decides momentarily not to marry him. In the *Ibrahim,* when Justinian must depart from Genoa after a six-month leave of absence from Soliman's service, Isabelle asserts a desire to follow him back to Constantinople that summarizes the conventional roles heroines play in the Heliodoran novel:

> Resist me not, Justiniano, unless you desire to offend me; suffer me to follow you with honour, and put me in the condition of increasing the number of those indiscreet ones, who many times have followed their Lovers, without being their wives. Think of my glory, I conjure you; and think too, that if you abandon me, I may be peradventure capable of forgetting it. Do not expose me, I beseech you, to that perill, since it is greater for me, according to my apprehensions, than the dreadfullest tempest that you can describe unto me. And fear not, I pray you either shipwrack or Pirats; if we perish together, we shall die almost without grief; if we be slaves, you will help me to bear my chains; of if we be separated, the fury of those barbarians shall do no more, than what you would do now. (*Ibrahim,* 145-46)

Desiring to be numbered among the "indiscreet ones, who many times followed their Lovers, without being their wives," Isabelle is self-conscious of her role as a romance heroine. She is willing to suffer tempests, shipwrecks, pirates, enslavements, even death and separation—all to assert the strength of her fidelity and her love.

The hero in the Heliodoran novel is generally less interesting than the heroine, perhaps because in trying to create epics of love, the authors found it necessary to curtail masculine heroism. Amyot's principal complaint about the *Aethiopica,* for example, is that the hero performs no memorable feats of arms.[17] While Theagenes wins the games at Delphos, becomes Thyamis's champion, and, at the end, subdues the rampant bull and defeats the Ethiopian champion, his heroic actions are peripheral to the plot. Imitating Heliodorus, Cervantes also subordinates his hero's physical prowess to his qualities as a faithful lover. In the heroic novels, there is considerably more attention to military adventures; Cyrus, for instance, becomes the conqueror of the world. Nevertheless, the motivating force behind many of Cyrus's conquests is his love for Mandane.

Matters of theme generally center around the wish fulfillment spirit that guides all romance. The love that seems sanctioned by the gods when the hero and heroine meet is subject to the earthly travails that make us wish for their happiness. When the lovers arrive at their destination and finally overcome all obstacles, the designs of providence are fulfilled, and one enters, figuratively, into the purifying realm of romance mythology.

In addition, the diversity in unity of the Heliodoran novel permits the development of more topical themes. Amyot and others praised the *Aethiopica* for its erudition, its encyclopedic inclusion of "noble discourses on moral and natural philosophy." The *Persiles,* as Alban K. Forcione notes, is a Counter-Reformation allegory of the journey of man.[18] The lovers travel from the barbarous North—where the true faith "had a little erred"—to Rome, the center of Roman Catholic civilization. In the *Ibrahim* and the *Cyrus,* the principal thematic elements are honor and decorum. Although removed in time and place from seventeenth-century France, these "speaking Pictures" (Scudéry, 3) reflect the genteel ideals about art, dress, customs, and conversations that are part and parcel of the *salons.*

Choices of style are integral with action, character, and theme. To heighten suspense and to exalt characters, there are numerous rhetorical pauses in which the heroes and heroines vent the ardor of their love, the cruelty of fortune, and their desperation at hearing of their lover's supposed death or infidelity. Elaborate recitals at the reunion of lovers allow offstage heroics to unfold in the suspenseful way the larger story line unfolds. These recitals and the lengthy histories of companions on the journey are often interrupted by the narrative necessitities of the plot, thus creating delight both in the story line and in the interpolations. There are highly stylized physical descriptions of the lovers, of battles, and of the places they visit. Above all, there is a pervasive consciousness about rhetorical embellishment: epic similes, periphrastic descriptions of dawn or evening, and parenthetical asides by the narrator about the villainy of rivals or about ominous events that occur.

In the heroic novels particularly, matters of style became so ornate that the embellishments themselves were a principal source of delight. One example—Justinian's recollection of his first sight of Isabelle—catches the flavor of the rest:

> she hath a stature so advantagious, and a port so majestical, as never was there woman seen of better presence. Her hair is of colour brown, but so beautiful, as all those threads of burnished gold, wherewith our Poets use to describe such, cannot represent them; they fell that day carelessly upon her cheeks, and thence descended in thick curls down her neck and bosome, but with a negligence so replenished with address, that it defaced the handsomest curiosity of all the women of the Assembly. She hath a complexion so white and vive, as there is no whiteness that seems not sallow unto it; but the same is mingled with so dainty a Carnation, which is shed abroad in her cheeks, that the mixture of Lillies and Roses, of Cynoper and Snow, could make but a slight Idea of her beauty. Her eyes are black, but so full of spirit and sweetnesse, as it is impossible to behold her, and not be taken with them; yet are her looks so modest, and so far from all artifice, as it is very easie to know they are innocent of all the evils

which they make one endure. She hath a mouth neither too great
nor too little, but so composed, and of so Vermillion a hew, as there
is no Corral that comes near it. Her teeth are so evenly set, and
so white, as never were smiles so full of charmes as her; and her
bosome so delicate and so comely, as imagination cannot represent
it selfe such as it is: there is also a gracefulness mingled amongst
all these marvels, which cannot be exprest, and which renders her
more amiable than all that which I delivered. To conclude, be it for
the whole form of the face, or for all the features of it in particular,
or for the air in general, it is the most perfect beauty that Nature
produced. (*Ibrahim,* 18)

The emphasis on clichéd comparisons with flowers and jewels, and
on hyperbolic expressions of a beauty that surpasses poetic imagination,
perfectly accord with a novel form in which the art is not so much
to imitate nature as to refine it, to poeticize it. We shall see blazons
of the heroes and heroines in Fielding's novels, which follow the
same pattern.

Curiously, it is the stylization itself that most appealed to the
salon readers, and yet this was the principal source of ridicule by
comic romancers like Scarron and Fielding. As we shall see, however,
even when these two comic romancers mock stylistic conventions,
they are fully conscious of integrating that mockery with the more
important elements of action and character.

3

A Comic Interlude:
Scarron's *Roman Comique*

Although works such as the *Grand Cyrus* remained popular in
England well into the eighteenth century, the literary tradition that
stems from Heliodorus's *Aethiopica* ends with the French heroic novels
in the mid-seventeenth century. Just as writers in the Heliodoran
tradition sought to correct excesses of structure and probability by
following the rules of the epic, so writers in the new tradition of
realism sought to correct excesses of convention in earlier romances.
Stylized conventions of the epic in prose were replaced by an increasing
emphasis on psychological development of characters, on more natural
settings and events, and on narrative forms that created the illusion
of reality, such as memoir-novels and epistolary novels.[1] Because of
this shift toward realism, the distinctive features of the Heliodoran
tradition became subsumed within the general pool of romance
literature. When Heliodoran features emerge in Fielding's novels,
they do so largely because Fielding drew much of his comedy, as
Cervantes did in *Don Quixote,* from the literary traditions that preceded
him.

   In chapters 4, 5, and 6 I shall demonstrate that despite Fielding's
comic use of many romance conventions, the very structure of his
three major novels parallels the structure and conventions of the
Heliodoran novel. But before we focus on these parallels, we should
consider a work that is directly linked to that tradition and that
influenced Fielding: Paul Scarron's *Roman Comique* (1651-57). This novel
is important for three reasons. First, it is directly a product of the

41

heroic-novel tradition in that it burlesques many of the excesses of style and conventionality found in the novels of La Calprenède, Scudéry, and others.[2] Second, the *Roman Comique* anticipates many of the comic-romance techniques that Fielding exploits in *Joseph Andrews* and *Tom Jones* and that Fielding and Scarron share with the comic tradition of *Don Quixote*.[3] Like Cervantes' narrator, for instance, both Scarron's and Fielding's narrators are self-consciously aware of their own status as narrators and, as a result, of their own literary agency; they comment frequently on the rhetoric of their creations, calling attention to the absurdity of serious conventions that they exploit. Third, by following the tradition of the heroic novel, Scarron exploits the narrative formula of the Heliodoran novel for comic purposes. In this respect, Scarron anticipates Fielding's exploitation of a similar formula in his comic romances.

The Roman Comique *and the Heliodoran Structure*

The *Roman Comique* deals with the adventures of a troupe of actors journeying through France. The action predominantly consists of comic adventures in a low style: numerous tavern brawls, dousings with chamber pots, and an assortment of tricks found in comic literature generally and in the picaresque particularly. Many episodes concern the vanities and affectations of Ragotin, a dwarfish lawyer accompanying the players, who is abused, mocked, and otherwise made the butt of several pranks by his companions. Scarron's work, however, is not entirely a novel in the low style. Blended into the comic incidents, framing them in fact, is a romance plot that constitutes the story-stuff of the novel and follows the distinctive pattern of the Heliodoran novel.

Like the Heliodoran novel, the *Roman Comique* begins in the middle of the action, with the players' arrival at the town of Mans. Initially, we are given no authorial explanation, but we quickly learn that some calamities in the antecedent action have brought the players to the town. We learn in chapter 2 of part I that their destination is Alençon and that they had to leave Tours, their last stop, because of some misfortune. As the beginning sequence develops and the characters are presented, we learn that one of the principal characters, named Destiny, is disguised in order to "make his Face unknown to some Enemies he had."[4] We learn a couple of chapters later that Destiny's dilemma resembles the conventional problem of the hero in the beginning of the Heliodoran novel. Rancour, another of the players (whose name reveals his disposition), makes the following observation about Destiny:

> Now he's lik'd because he is young; but if you knew him throughly as I do, you would not have so good an Opinion of him; Besides he is as proud, as if he was lineally Descended from Saint Lewis, and yet he won't tell us who he is, nor whence he comes, no more than a handsom Phillis who accompanied him, under the name of Sister, and grant Heaven she be no worse. (Scarron, 10)

Although Rancour is skeptical here of Destiny's noble status, he does provide a comic perspective from which we can see three typical conventions of the Heliodoran novel: the hero's nobility, the heroine's beauty, and their disguise as brother and sister.

As we might expect, the pattern of action connected with Destiny and Star (the heroine) follows the four phases of the Heliodoran novel. The first phase, as is conventional, is revealed by Destiny's narrative recital in the middle of the present action (pt. I, chaps. 13, 15, and 18). We learn of Destiny's birth, his love for the heroine (whose real name is Leonora), her mother's objection to their marriage, Destiny's forced departure to serve in the Pope's army (an incident that recalls Justinian's departure in the *Ibrahim*), and the lovers' agreement to meet in France.

Phase two consists of a variety of offstage adventures reported by narrative recitals and also the comic displacement of other adventures in the present action. In the offstage action, the heroine is pursued by a villainous lover, Saldagne, from whose assault Destiny had defended the heroine when he and Star first met. Saldagne serves as the recurrent threat throughout the novel; it is his presence at Alençon that forced the players to travel to Mans, and it is he who abducts the heroine during the present action of the novel.

In addition to the complications presented by this rival, there are also complications posed by the heroine's mother. Like Isabelle's mother in the *Ibrahim,* Star's mother objects to her daughter's love for the hero and arranges for her to marry a suitor of nobler birth. This parental threat, however, is removed shortly after Destiny rejoins Leonora in France. News arrives that Leonora's father has been banished from the court, rendering the heroine and her mother penniless. Destiny, however, acts as their protector and they travel together. During their journey the heroine's mother loses an enameled box, encrusted with diamonds, that contains a picture of the heroine's father. This serves as the conventional possession—not unlike Chariclea's silken ribbon or Auristela's diamond crucifix—that will eventually reveal the heroine's identity.[5] Eventually, the heroine's mother dies, and the lovers join a group of traveling players under the disguised identities of Destiny and Star. In this company the lovers encounter the same sorts of threats that characterize the Heliodoran novel: at Tours, the city the players had visited immediately before the novel begins, they again meet with Saldagne, necessitating a hasty departure during which the lovers are separated. When the lovers are reunited in the present action, they undergo stock adventures of Heliodoran-novel protagonists: the heroine is courted by one of their companions, Ragotin; a subordinate set of lovers, Leander and Angelica, undergo adventures that complement those of the hero and heroine; the heroine is abducted, and the hero pursues her.

A great deal of the present action, however, is given over to the comic antics of the players, and in these actions Scarron comically displaces the serious-romance conventions of the Heliodoran novel. Saldagne's pursuit of Star, for instance, follows a pattern typical of serious romance, but this rivalry is comically balanced by that of the dwarfish lawyer, Ragotin, whose pining for the heroine precipitates further low humor, such as a serenade in which all the mongrels of the town join his musicians in a yelping chorus. Even the hero's serious-romance role is counterbalanced by comic action. Like Theagenes, Periandro, and Cyrus, Destiny inadvertently wins the affections of an amorous gentlewoman, Mme. Bouvillon. Yet she, unlike Arsace, Hipólita, or Queen Thomiris, is bovine and lustful— a prototype of Mrs. Slipslop. And Destiny, unlike the conventional hero, is all too willing to accede to her charms.

These comic twists to the romance pattern clearly advance Scarron's burlesque of the heroic-novel tradition, yet at the same time they transfer the value of earlier conventions into a new form. Ragotin's love for Star, in a serious romance, would serve to heighten suspense, to add a further complication to the plot. But because his affections are so absurd and because they provide comic relief for the romanesque elements in the novel, they provide a different sort of suspense.

Phases Three and Four: the Suite D'Offray

Since Scarron only completed two parts of the *Roman Comique,* his version leaves the narrative thread dangling roughly at the end of the second phase. The novel was continued by at least three others, the most famous of whom is Antoine Offray. The *Suite D'Offray* is clearly inferior to Scarron's novel, yet Offray brings the two sets of lovers to the type of complications we expect in phase three and to a displaced version of the happy ending we expect in phase four.

In phase three, Offray's lovers arrive in Alençon after a series of complications, during which Star is rescued from her abductor, Saldagne. The lovers endure a final confrontation with Saldagne, defeat him, and face the further complication of being unable to secure a marriage license. Eventually, this difficulty is overcome, and their marriage follows.

Unlike the Heliodoran novel, however, the lovers are not restored to their true identities. In Offray's version, the couple chooses to stay with the traveling company under their assumed names. In fact, their marriage does not, as we would expect, conclude the novel. Instead we are given two more interpolated novellas and a comic sequence in which Ragotin is distraught at Star's marriage, attempts suicide, composes his own epitaph, and then accidentally drowns. The serious-romance pattern is thus completed, yet its conventional effect is displaced by antiromance events. Instead of the ideal ritual marriage that promises a future of divinely promised bliss, the hero and heroine choose an earthly path. Although Saldagne is punished as poetic justice dictates, the comic rival, Ragotin, suffers an end that is capricious, if not unduly cruel. The effect is to infuse a sense of irresolution in a pattern that we expect to be providentially resolved.

Scarron, Fielding, and Comic-Romance Conventions

Although Fielding exploits the materials of romance in a way different from Scarron, his self-conscious narrative pose owes part of its allegiance to Scarron. Indeed, this self-consciousness makes us aware of the literary rules that are being reshaped for the comic romance.

In the opening of part I, chapter 12, Scarron mocks the principles of unity, decorum, instruction, and delight that were so highly esteemed by writers in the Heliodoran novel tradition:

> I am too much a Man of Honour not to advertise the Courteous Reader, that if he be offended at all the silly Trifles he has already seen in this present Book, he will do well not to go on with the reading of it; for, upon my Conscience, he must expect nothing else, altho' the Book shou'd swell to the bigness of the *Grand Cyrus:* And if from what he has read, he doubts what will follow, perhaps I am in the same Doubt as he: for one Chapter draws on another, and I do with my Book as some do with their Horses they bestride, having the Bridle on their Neck, and trusting to their good Conduct. But perhaps I have a fix'd Design, and without filling my Books with Examples for Imitation, I shall instruct with Delight in the same manner as

> a drunken Man creates in us an Aversion for Drunkenness, and may
> sometimes divert us by his merry Impertinences. (Scarron, 40)

Although the disavowal of art here ridicules the artifice of romance conventions, Scarron directs our attention to what we should expect but are not getting. We should expect serious adventures, not trifles; we should expect the author to have those adventures in narrative rein, however large the book swells; we should expect instruction and delight that come from an elevation of the subject matter and a sober control over that matter's disposition. By disavowing control, Scarron frees the reader from his or her romance expectations, but, at the same time, programs the reader to expect a comic fulfillment of disavowed promises.

In a similar way, Scarron debunks the rhetorical embellishments that characterize the heroic novels. In doing so, he attacks the literary ideals on which the Heliodoran novel is based. In aspiring to the epic, the Heliodoran novelists used many of the stylistic devices of epic poetry: hyperbolic descriptions, heroic similes and analogies, lengthy periphrastic descriptions of dawn or evening, intricate recitals of antecedent or off-stage action.

Scarron's very opening chapter burlesques several romance embellishments. It opens with a traditional periphrastic description:[6]

> Bright Phoebus had already perform'd above half his Career; and his Chariot having past the Meridian, and got on the Declivity of the Sky, roll'd on swifter than he desir'd. Had his Horses been willing to make use of the slopingness of the Way, they might have finished the remainder of the Day in less than half a quarter of an Hour: But instead of pulling amain, they curvetted about, snuffing a Briny Air, which set them a neighing, and made them sensible that they were near the Sea, where their Father is said to take his Rest every Night. To speak more like a Man, and in plainer Terms; it was betwixt five and six of the clock, when a Cart came into the Marketplace of Mans. (Scarron, 1)

The burlesque technique here is clear: the first sentence invites us to expect a rhetorical cliché; the second sentence complicates the cliché with the image of recalcitrant horses; in the third sentence, the narrator jerks us from the celestial sphere of Phoebus to the world of men who speak in plainer terms. By stopping the flourish in mid-stride, however, the narrator emphasizes the curtailed romance rhetoric.

Fielding employs a similar technique in the opening of book 1, chapter 8 of *Joseph Andrews:*

Now the Rake Hesperus had called for his Breeches, and having well
rubbed his drowsy Eyes, prepared to dress himself for all Night; by
whose Example his Brother Rakes on Earth likewise leave those Beds,
in which they had slept away the Day. Now Thetis the good Housewife
began to put on the Pot in order to regale the good Man Phoebus,
after his daily Labours were over. In vulgar Language, it was in the
Evening when Joseph attended his Lady's Orders. (*Joseph Andrews*, 37-
38)

Here the mockery of the convention works by an imaginative
substitution of contemporary types for mythological figures: Hesperus,
the evening star, is a rake calling for his breeches and awakening
earthly rakes for an evening's romp, while Phoebus is regaled with
a Pot after his labors. It is fundamentally a vulgarized hyperbole
that is perfectly appropriate for the disparity between Lady Booby's
pretended gentility and her lust for Joseph.

Later in Scarron's opening chapter it becomes clear that his
narrator, like Fielding's, is conscious of the reader's sense of literary
decorum. In describing one of the musicians in the company, he sets
up a simple, albeit low, simile: "He carried a Base-viol over his
Shoulders; and because he stoop'd a little as he went along, one might
have taken him at a distance for a great Tortoise walking on his
hind-Feet" (Scarron, 2). The image is vivid enough for the world
of plain-speaking humans, but in an intrusive commentary on the
comparison, the narrator calls our attention to the literary rules that
are mocked:

Some Critick or other will perhaps find fault with the Comparison,
by reason of the Disproportion between a Tortoise and a Man: But
I speak of those great Tortoises that are found in the Indies; and besides,
I make bold to use the Simile upon my own Authority. (Scarron,
2)

Like Fielding's, Scarron's comic rhetoric forces readers to reassess
their sense of literary criticism. Scarron's disgust, of course, is simply
with the authority of literary decorum, while Fielding, particularly
in *Tom Jones*, offers a more elaborate commentary on literary rules.
Yet the germ of Fielding's comic-epic rhetoric is very similar to
Scarron's.

In its less intrusive moments, Scarron's opening chapter parodies
the kinds of technique found in the Heliodoran novel tradition. In
the *Aethiopica*, the *Persiles*, and the *Grand Cyrus*, the reader is thrust
into the middle of a dramatically tense scene that immediately produces
suspense. In the *Roman Comique*, after the periphrastic opener, we
are introduced to a procession of players and the scuffle that ensues

upon their entrance into the town. Although not so suspenseful as
the Heliodoran novel, this *in medias res* opener does prompt us to
expect further information about the players. Indeed, the procession
recalls the opening of the *Ibrahim,* in which we get a description
of the pomp and ceremony of the Sultan's entrance into Constantinople:

> Scarcely had the first beames of the Sun dissipated the darkness of
> the Night on the Bosphorus of Thrace, when as a great voyce of
> Trumpets and Atabales awaked every one in the Imperial City of
> Constantinople, and made them know that the Triumph of great Soliman
> was beginning. (*Ibrahim,* 170)

After describing Soliman and his entourage, Scudéry gives us a lush
description of the hero:

> Behind them Ibrahim Bassa, the Grand Visier, rode alone, mounted
> on a blacke Barbe, whose furniture was velvet, of the same colour
> as well as the habit of that illustrious Bassa, all imbroidered with
> great pearls, he carried in his hand, and without a scabbard, the Scymitar
> Imperial. (*Ibrahim,* 2)

Scarron's description inverts the kind of pomp and ceremony
of Ibrahim's entrance. The company of players has a cart "drawn
by two Yokes of lean Oxen, led by a breeding Mare, who had a
Calf that skipp'd to and fro about the Cart, like a silly Creature
as he was" (Scarron, 1). As with the tortoiselike bass-violist, the
animals, not the ceremony, draw our attention. Then we are presented
with our hero, Destiny, who is described in terms that inversely
parallel those in Scudéry's novel:

> A young man, as poor in Cloaths, as rich in Mien, walk'd by the
> side of the Cart: He had a great Patch on his Face, (which covered
> one of his Eyes, and half of one Cheek) and carried a long Birding
> piece over his Shoulder, wherewith he had murdered several Magpies,
> Jayes, and Crows, which made a sort of Bandileer; at the bottom
> of which hung a Hen and a Goose, that look'd as if they had been
> taken from the Enemy by way of Plunder. Instead of a Hat he wore
> a Night-Cap, tied about his Head with Garters of several Colours;
> and this Headdress was without a doubt a kind of unfinish'd Turbant.
> His Doublet was a Griset-Coat, girt over with a Leather Thong; which
> serv'd likewise to support a Rapier so very long, that it could not
> be us'd dextrously without the help of a Rest. He wore a pair of
> Breaches tuck'd up to above the middle of his Thighs, like those that
> Players wear when they represent an ancient Hero; and instead of
> shoes he wore Tragick Buskins, which were bespatter'd with Dirt
> up to the Ancles. (Scarron, 1-2)

Unlike Ibrahim, who rides a "black Barbe," Destiny walks. Destiny's weaponry, instead of the unscabbarded "Scymitar Imperial," suggests a poacher rather than a conqueror. In contrast to the richly embroidered velvet of Scudéry's hero, Scarron's sports a motley nightcap (which interestingly enough resembles a turban), a Griset-Coat finished off with leather thongs, and soiled buskins. Yet, that Destiny is as poor in garb as he is rich in mien suggests the conventional situation of the disguised Heliodoran-novel hero. Indeed, Ibrahim, though rich in garb, is poor in spirit—having been separated from his love.

The opening chapter thus prepares us for a novel that reflects the kind of serious romance found in the Heliodoran tradition but shatters its fragile conventions. Instead of a superfluity of valiant deeds by exalted characters, we are presented with a near-romance hero and heroine whose adventures are overshadowed by the slapstick, antiromance characters.

Comic-Romance Embellishments and Chapter Divisions

Two other features of Scarron's work anticipate the kind of comic rhetoric Fielding employs in *Joseph Andrews* and *Tom Jones:* a comic exploitation of narrative recitals and capricious divisions of chapters. Neither are unique to Scarron (Cervantes tinkers with both devices), yet these two devices reinforce the reader's consciousness of the literary conventions being violated.

Typically in the Heliodoran novel, the principal narrative line is interrupted by lengthy recitals of offstage or antecedent action. In the *Aethiopica,* for instance, Calasiris's history of the hero and heroine before the opening scene of the novel stretches from book 2 to book 5—a little over one third of the work. For the novelists imitating Heliodorus, this narrative technique became a means of embellishment. Not only did heroes and heroines recount their adventures—recreating for the other the danger and despair they experienced—but companions on the journey also frequently told their own histories. The purpose of these interruptions is to provide love stories that are thematically analogous to the hero's and heroine's, and, probably more important, to divert the reader with miniature histories, many of which can be read in one sitting without taxing one's memory of the larger plot line.

Scarron burlesques this convention in two ways. First, he capriciously interrupts Destiny's narrative recital with the comic antics of the players. As the hero begins his history, having evoked a few sympathetic tears from his listeners, he is interrupted by a brawl in the tavern-room below. He investigates and joins in the fracas. When he rebegins his history, he is interrupted twice more—first because of the lateness of the hour, then because of Ragotin's comic serenade of Star. Thus, as we are prepared to be diverted by a serious-romance recital, we are diverted by comic adventures.

Second, Scarron often substitutes novellas for narrative recitals. Cervantes, of course, does the same thing in *Don Quixote*. But in a work that otherwise burlesques heroic novel conventions, this substitution is probably also burlesque in nature. In the *Ibrahim* and the *Cyrus,* many of the recitals are delivered by characters who have, at best, a peripheral connection to the plot; generally these recitals assume the guise of history, but their primary function seems to be entertainment. By inserting overtly fictional stories into the conventional formula, Scarron further reinforces his criticism of the empty literary conventions of serious romance—suggesting, perhaps, that serious romance takes its allegiance to history a bit too seriously.

Scarron's capricious chapter divisions and chapter titles also remind one not to take this romance too seriously; indeed, they often direct our attention to the author's self-conscious pose. Scarron writes a book rather than a romance. In the heroic novels, the innumerable volumes are usually divided into long, monolithic parts; Scarron's chapters are typically short and divided whimsically.[7] He concludes the opening chapter, for instance, by noting that, while the beasts that drew the players' cart were feeding, "the Author rested a while, and bethought himself what he could say in the next Chapter" (Scarron, 3). This technique not only emphasizes a caprice of transition, but in doing so it undermines the suspense we should feel after an *in medias res* opener. At other points Scarron comments, tongue in cheek, on the content of the chapter he has written. He concludes 1.11, for example, by noting that he has "sufficiently exercis'd" our patience with "a tedious Story of Ragotin's Debauch" and proposes to return to the players' inn (Scarron, 40).

One can readily see how Fielding follows Scarron's footsteps in 2.1 of *Joseph Andrews*—a dissertation on "Divisions in Authors." The mysterious craft of dividing works into books and chapters, despite the recondite efforts of critics to search for rules for dividing, is simply a matter of practicality: "it becomes an Author generally to divide a Book, as it doth a Butcher to joint his Meat, for such Assistance is of great help to the Reader and the Carver" (*Joseph Andrews,* 92). Indeed, like Scarron's, Fielding's narrator often comments, tongue in cheek, on presenting too large a joint for the reader's patient carving.[8]

A self-consciousness about divisions carries over into a more external self-consciousness in chapter titles. Many of Scarron's titles, like Fielding's, are simply informative, but occasionally both authors direct our attention to the romance matter being exploited. Book 2.11 of the *Roman Comique,* for example, interrupts Mme. Bouvillon's comic seduction of Destiny with the story of how Angelica was rescued from her abduction, how Star has been abducted, and how Destiny meets with Vervelle, an ally against Saldagne. The chapter title ironically stresses these romance adventures by denying its entertainment value: "Of things that will divert, it may be, the least of the whole Book" (Scarron, 186). In the following chapter—"Which perhaps will entertain its Readers as little as the foregoing" (Scarron, 190)—Vervelle tells Destiny that Saldagne is Star's abductor and helps the hero rescue the heroine. The title, thus deemphasizing romance material, encourages the reader to view the work with two sets of critical eyes: one set is diverted only by the comic antics of the players; the other is diverted by the ongoing romance adventures, but must mask—as it were—the pleasure it takes in that diversion.

Fielding uses a similar technique, yet adds to Scarron's a more explicit separation of romance and antiromance readers. In 5.3 of *Tom Jones,* for instance, the hero suffers through an internal debate between his love for Sophia and his obligations toward the pregnant Molly. The chapter's title—"Which all, who have no Heart, will think to contain much adoe about nothing"—emphasizes litotically the good hearted reader's diversion and the ill-natured reader's impatience with material that does not bring the hero to a hanging.

Conclusion

The tradition of literary burlesque and literary self consciousness that influences Scarron and Fielding certainly owes much to Cervantes' comic manner. Yet Scarron departs from Cervantes in some very important ways, and that departure, I would argue, affects Fielding's new province of comic-romance writing. Both Scarron and Cervantes chide readers who take the clichés of romance too seriously yet know better. Through the Canon of Toledo, Cervantes offers a corrective. He criticizes romances of chivalry and establishes the rules for an ideal epic in prose. Scarron proposes no extensive literary debate, nor any ideal substitute. Rather, he embeds antiromance material within a romance formula. The juxtaposition of the two inevitably gives the *Roman Comique* the flavor of burlesque, yet the juxtaposition also effects a synthesis that Fielding will later refine.

4

The Romance Structure of *Joseph Andrews*

If we ignore for the moment the love story of Joseph and Fanny, *Joseph Andrews* consists largely of two essentially different narrative veins: the *Pamela* material that gives the hero his name and the quixotic antics of Parson Adams.[1] The first programs us to expect a literary burlesque of Richardson's novel; the second shifts our attention from a parodic mode to a humorous mode. Together, both veins contain what is perhaps most vividly memorable about the novel: Lady Booby's seduction of Joseph, Mrs. Slipslop's malapropisms, Parson Adams's eccentric memory, his being doused with hog's blood, his naiveté about Christian charity, and his nocturnal misdirections at Lady Booby's. Yet if we wish to discuss the plot of the novel, neither of these two veins will fit the bill. The former leads one to conclude that the novel is an aborted burlesque; the latter, a shapeless quixotic romp.

It is only when we consider the love story that the novel takes any kind of coherent narrative form at all. It is Joseph's decision to return to Lady Booby's estate that shifts the novel away from the *Pamela* burlesque. It is Fanny's love for him that causes her to leave the parish and seek the hero. It is that quest which leads her path and that of Parson Adams to cross and leads eventually to her reunion with Joseph. It is Joseph's and Fanny's love, and the parson's adamantine insistence on posting their wedding banns, that give the journey a purpose. And it is that purpose which precipitates both Lady Booby's plot with Lawyer Scout to have Fanny arrested and Booby's unsuccessful plot with Beau Didapper to have Fanny raped. It is the hero's and heroine's love that heightens suspense when Fanny is revealed to be an Andrews, thus making Pamela—vain, snobbish, hypocritical—another Shamela. Finally, it is the wedding of Joseph and Fanny that ultimately resolves the novel. In short, it is essentially a romance plot that directs *Joseph Andrews* to its conclusion, even though that plot, especially during the comic medley of reversals at the end, seems more chaotic than controlled, more accidental than guided by narrative providence.

In order to see how this romance plot functions, we need to examine the shift in narrative direction that takes place in book 1, chapter 11, when Joseph, dismissed by Lady Booby, decides to return to the Booby estate instead of to his parents' home. From this point in the novel the plot begins to take on the appearance of a love story not unlike that in the Heliodoran novel. Indeed, with the "new Matters not expected" that Fielding provides about Joseph and Fanny's relationship, we get an *in media res* rebeginning of the novel in the midst of things. From 1.11 to the end of the novel, the love story of Joseph and Fanny is the most important structural element in the plot, and it provides a resolution to the *Pamela* burlesque with which the novel begins.

Romance and History in Joseph Andrews

Characteristically, the first phase of the Heliodoran novel is reported after the *in medias res* beginning: sometimes in one large chunk that brings the reader to understand all action up to the opening scene of the novel (as in the *Aethiopica,* the *Ibrahim,* and the *Cyrus*), sometimes in piecemeal accounts that are not fully revealed until the end (as in the *Persiles*). The purpose of this convention was both to follow perceived rules for the epic in prose and to create unity and suspense in works that were *similar* to truth but not truth itself. Although all narratives might be said to thrust one into the middle of things (the province of narrative being the world between "once upon a time" and "happily ever after"), this kind of beginning implies an immediate and a long-range set of complications. As Amyot points out, the structure makes us want to understand what has taken place before the characters were brought to the calamity with which the novel opens, and, when this desire is fulfilled, we are curious about how matters will be resolved.[2]

To construct a metaphor resembling Freytag's triangle, in an *in medias res* beginning we join characters who are dangling from a crag of a ragged mountainous slope that will lead, in its ascent, to a plateau and a resting point before we ascend higher and encounter further crags and complications. In the distance below—or as it were, behind us—we can see the gentle slope whence the journey began and the crags and plateaus that have brought us to this middle height in the ascending action. Since there is no way backward except to fall—in which case we would be in a tragic mode, not an epic or a romance mode—we have little choice but to ascend higher, surmount the highest peak, and descend by a gentler (and deceptively less dangerous) slope to the promised valley on the other side.

When Joseph Andrews decides in 1.11 to seek Fanny at Lady Booby's estate, we are, in effect, thrust into the middle of a journey whose terrain has so far not revealed the ascent we have been making. Up until that point in the novel, the kind of story we are programmed to expect is guided by what Fielding calls "history."

By "history" Fielding seems to imply not only that fictional mode, in contrast to "novels and romances," which owes its allegiance to truth, but also a particular habit of narrative that stresses the appearance of causality. It is ordered and arranged by a narrator who defines the relative importance and unimportance of the facts he presents.[3] This habit is broadly similar to the pose of "formal realism" by which Ian Watt characterizes the works of Defoe and Richardson.[4] Yet despite the essentially empirical pose that Fielding assumes by portraying events in a spatial and temporal world, the authentic report of human experience he presents is fundamentally not referential. The kind of "history" that Fielding creates in *Joseph Andrews* (and even more strikingly in *Tom Jones* and *Amelia*) might be better characterized as "causal-similar." That is, by professing an allegiance to empirical truth and by feigning an objectivity about the causal sequence of events, Fielding creates a likeness to causality. Like verisimilitude in the Heliodoran novel, it is not merely a referential report of events and their consequences, but also a rhetorical manipulation of characters and events.

In order to create the effect of causal similitude, Fielding's narrator frequently recounts events that occurred earlier, fills in or leaps over periods of time, and digresses analytically on the meaning of events or on the reader's inability to perceive those events properly. Instead of the "disguised" history we find in the Heliodoran tradition, we find in Fielding's novels a "designed" history: fiction that stresses the immediacy of events, their flux and contingency, instead of a foreseeable order. The emphasis, at least until we fully understand the author's design, is on a horizontal or episodic narrative line rather than on the vertical ascent of romance. In *Tom Jones* Fielding manages to blend the rhetoric of history or causal similitude so carefully with the romance rhetoric that we do not fully understand the romance pattern until the novel is ended. In *Joseph Andrews,* however, the two are not reconciled so deftly; as a result, the shift that takes place in 1.11 calls attention to an almost naive romance plot.

Although the narrator assumes the pose of a historian by attempting to fill in the informational gap about Joseph's and Fanny's relationship (he goes as far as explaining that the two have not corresponded because Fanny cannot read), his description of the hero's and heroine's love emphasizes sensation rather than information: "Nothing can be imagined more tender than was the parting between these Lovers. A thousand Sighs heaved the Bosom of Joseph; a thousand Tears distilled from the lovely Eyes of Fanny" (*Joseph Andrews*, 49). The confessed inability of the historian to describe their parting, combined with the hyperbolic enumeration of their thousand sighs and tears, compresses the stylized descriptions of parting that would normally be embellished at great length in the Heliodoran novel. The result is a romance scene qualified by the historian's empirical pose.

As the passage continues, Fielding blends romance cliché with empirical observation:

> Tho' her Modesty would only suffer her to admit his eager Kisses, her violent Love made her more than passive in his Embraces; and she often pulled him to her Breast with a soft Pressure, which tho' perhaps it would not have squeezed an Insect to death, caused more Emotion in the Heart of Joseph, than the closest Cornish Hug could have done. (*Joseph Andrews*, 49)

By measuring Fanny's soft embrace against the more realistic grappling of Cornish wrestlers, Fielding indirectly emphasizes the sentimental romance rhetoric of the scene without embellishing it. Later on in the chapter, the narrator blends a hyperbolic metaphor with a causal-similar description:

> Those who have read any Romance or Poetry antient or modern, must have been informed, that Love hath Wings; by which they are not to understand, as some young Ladies by mistake have done, that a Lover can fly: the Writers, by this ingenious Allegory, intending to insinuate no more, than that Lovers do not march like Horse-Guards; in short, that they put the best Leg foremost, which our lusty Youth, who could walk with any Man, did so heartily on this occasion, that within four Hours, he reached a famous House of Hospitality well known to the western Traveller. (*Joseph Andrews*, 49)

Fielding's strategy here is to move us from the metaphoric language of romance and poetry to the realm of plain speaking men who measure time by hours and who identify geographical locations by recognizable signs. The explanation of the cliché resembles Scarron's frequent commentaries on figurative language, but the commentary takes on a peculiar twist here. It is directed to those who *must have been informed* by romance or poetry that love has wings—that is, to readers capable of a romance imagination even in an empirically ordered narrative. In effect, Fielding urges us to read, as it were, both the signs of history and the signs of romance.

From 1.11 to the conclusion, romance suggestions that ultimately resemble the Heliodoran pattern coexist with causal similitude. When Joseph is attacked on the road, the narrative immediately shifts back to causal similitude. Yet, if we consider the action relevant to the hero's and heroine's reunion and journey back to the country, the plot follows the four phases of action in the Heliodoran novel.

Joseph Andrews *and the Heliodoran Structure*

The first phase, the initial love of the hero and heroine, is compressed in the information we receive in 1.11. There we learn that Joseph and Fanny have loved each other to such a degree that Parson Adams, like Calasiris in the *Aethiopica,* had "with much ado prevented them from marrying" (*Joseph Andrews*, 48). We learn also that even in their separation they relied on a "mutual Confidence in each other's Fidelity, and the Prospect of their future Happiness" (*Joseph Andrews*, 49), much like the hero and heroine of the Heliodoran novel when they are separated.

The ritual of their betrothal, which I see as an essential ingredient in the first phase of the Heliodoran novel, does not take place until 2.13, after Joseph and Fanny are reunited—an incident I would place in phase two. Yet it is not unusual in some novels, such as the *Persiles,* for the lovers to reiterate their vows during the journey. Indeed, in the *Persiles* this reiteration alerts us to the purpose of the journey: the heroine's purification in Rome. In a work like *Joseph Andrews,* where causal similitude dominates the plot, the formal betrothal in the middle of the present action of the novel makes logical sense, for it then defines a causal purpose for the ensuing journey.

The second phase conventionally consists of the journey of the lovers, their separations, and their reunions, as well as the abductions, conflicts with rivals, and other accidents that occur while they are together and apart. All of these test the lovers' fidelity and threaten to keep them from their destination. Typically, we enter the novel in the middle of the second phase; the lovers are separated, and one or the other is placed in jeopardy. Such an event occurs in *Joseph Andrews* by virtue of Joseph's dismissal from Lady Booby's service and his attack by highwaymen. After Joseph is taken to the Towwouse inn, where he meets with Parson Adams, Fanny hears a rumor, not unlike that which Mandane hears in the *Cyrus,* that the hero is mortally injured.[5] Fanny then ventures out to find Joseph, while he is journeying to the country to be reunited with her. Because of the causal-similar logic of the plot, we do not learn of Fanny's quest until much later, but when we do (in 2.10), the information follows a scene that very much resembles a romance calamity: she has been rescued by Adams from a ravisher.[6] When Joseph and Fanny are reunited in 2.12 (notably after the narrator's embellished description of Fanny), they agree to wait until they return to Parson Adams's parish before they wed. The destination and purpose of the journey are thus clearly defined. The hero and heroine, from that point on, are betrothed lovers, and Adams assumes the combined roles of priest, father figure, intermediary, and friendly guide—all the roles that Calasiris assumes in the *Aethiopica.*

The journey of the lovers from 2.13 to the end of book 3 follows many of the conventions of the Heliodoran novel. Although there are no shipwrecks as in the Heliodoran-novel tradition, the pecuniary dilemmas of Joseph, Fanny, and Adams at various inns displace these accidents and permit Fielding to develop the theme of charity that pervades the novel.[7] Like the lovers and their companions in the Heliodoran novel, our travelers meet with several characters: some friendly, such as the Wilsons (whose history serves a function analogous to Renato's in the *Persiles*;[8] some unfriendly, such as the hunting squire. Indeed, the latter, through the agency of the Captain, abducts the heroine, causing the hero to react with a rhetorical complaint against providence—a conventional pause in the action that builds suspense while the heroine is transferred from one villain (the Captain) to another (Peter Pounce) before she is reunited with Joseph and Adams.[9]

The third phase, the lovers' arrival at their destination and the final complications, comprises the entirety of book 4. Although the path seems clear for their marriage, Lady Booby, like Arsace in the *Aethiopica* and Hipólita in the *Persiles,* plots with Lawyer Scout and later with Beau Didapper against Fanny.[10] The major complications of this phase, however, concern the mysteries of Joseph's and Fanny's identities, and with them, Fielding manipulates suspense as Heliodorus and his followers do. Fanny is first revealed to be an Andrews, and thus supposedly Joseph's sister, ironically recalling the conventional disguise of the Heliodoran-novel hero and heroine as brother and sister. At this point the wished-for happy ending seems utterly impossible, but the complications are resolved when Joseph's parentage is revealed. In the *Aethiopica* and the *Persiles,* the final complications are devices of suspense: we know that the hero and heroine are betrothed lovers, not brother and sister; the revelation of their identities thus does not surprise us. In Fielding's novel the lovers appear to be brother and sister until they are recognized as lovers once again. It is almost as though Fielding comically inverts the conventional disguise in order to effect a surprise ending.

The fourth phase, as in the Heliodoran novel, is a matter of ceremony: with the impediments removed, the banns can be published and the lovers marry.

Characters and the Heliodoran Novel

Just as the action of *Joseph Andrews,* when paralleled with the Heliodoran novel, demonstrates an intertwining of a romance plot with a causal-similar one, so matters of character and theme integrate the two modes. Indeed, by examining these in light of the Heliodoran pattern, we can see how Fielding uses the stylistic conventions of romance to emphasize the internal qualities of his principal characters.

In the Heliodoran novel, we are typically presented with a hero and a heroine, each chaste and faithful, each defined principally as a lover, who are conducted on their journey by a guide who is both a spiritual and an earthly father figure. Joseph, Fanny, and Adams embody these conventions, but they differ from them because they also reflect other literary influences.

Fanny's character is invested with little else but romance convention. She is distinguished by her beauty and her chastity, as are the heroines in the Heliodoran novel, but not by her nobility *per se.* Like Chariclea and Auristela, Fanny's beauty makes her the object of desire of several villainous characters in the novel. She is attacked by an unnamed person on the road (2.11), by the Captain (3.9), and by Beau Didapper's servant (4.7). She even appears to be under attack when Parson Adams inadvertently ends up in her bed in 4.15. In each case, as in the Heliodoran novel, her virtue is protected by the providential arrival of either Adams or Joseph—or, in the last instance, by both.

Fanny's chastity defines her principal role in the novel, yet this role is qualified by the causal-similar pose the narrator assumes. The embellished description Fielding offers of her in 2.12 juxtaposes the clichés found in the highly ornamental embellishments of the Heliodoran novel with the more realistic details of Fielding's causal similitude. In introducing the heroine, Fielding comically toys with the rhetoric of romance embellishment by urging the reader "of an amorous Hue" to skip over the description. This sort of introduction prepares us not only for a conventional description, but also for a realistic rendering of it that might prompt us to fall in love with Fanny. The sketch itself begins in conventional terms but is qualified after each trope:

> she was tall and delicately shaped; but not one of those slender young Women, who seem rather intended to hang up in the Hall of an Anatomist, than for any other Purpose. On the contrary, she was so plump, that she seemed bursting through her tight Stays, especially in the Part which confined her swelling Breasts. Nor did her Hips want the Assistance of a Hoop to extend them. (*Joseph Andrews*, 152)

The first detail—her tall, delicate shape—is what we expect of a romance heroine, but Fielding rounds out her character, so to speak, in more robust terms. Indeed, the embellishment is made unconventional by her name: Fanny. As the sketch continues, Fielding uses the pattern of a blazon, not unlike the one that Scudéry uses in the *Ibrahim*:

> The exact Shape of her Arms denoted the Form of those Limbs which she concealed; and tho' they were a little redden'd by her Labour, yet if her Sleeve slipt above her Elbow, or her Handkerchief discovered any part of her Neck, a Whiteness appeared which the finest Italian Paint would be unable to reach. Her Hair was of a chestnut Brown, and Nature had been extremely lavish to her of it, which she had cut, and on Sundays used to curl down her Neck in the modern Fashion. Her Forehead was high, her Eye-brows arched, and rather full than otherwise. Her Eyes black and sparkling; her Nose, just inclining to the Roman; her Lips red and moist, and her Under-lip, according to the Opinion of the Ladies, too pouting. Her Teeth were white, but not exactly even. The Small-Pox had left only one Mark on her Chin, which was so large, it might have been mistaken for a Dimple, had not her left Cheek produced one so near a Neighbour to it, that the former seemed only a Foil to the latter. Her Complexion was fair, a little injured by the Sun, but overspread with such a Bloom, that the finest Ladies would have exchanged all their White for it: add to these, a Countenance in which tho' she was extremely bashful, a Sensibility appeared almost incredible; and a Sweetness, whenever she smiled, beyond either Imitation or Description. To conclude all,

> she had a natural Gentility, superiour to the Acquisition of Art, and
> which surprized all who beheld her. (*Joseph Andrews*, 152-53)

Such a description blends together comically realistic details (arms
reddened by labour, teeth "not exactly even," a smallpox blemish
on her chin, and a slightly sunburnt complexion) with the hyperboles
of romance embellishment (a whiteness surpassing the finest Italian
paint, a sensibility almost incredible, a smile beyond imitation or
description). The frame of the portrait invites such clichéd comparison
as hairs like golden wires and teeth like pearls, yet Fielding consciously
avoids these. By juxtaposing conventional and unconventional
elements, Fielding does not debunk romance cliché but redefines it.
Fanny has a "natural Gentilty, superiour to the Acquistion of Art"
that surprises all who behold her because, in its very naturalness,
it evokes a quality akin to the exalted beauty of heroines in more
conventional romances.

Like the heroines in the *Aethiopica* and the *Persiles,* Fanny's beauty
and inner gentility make her attractive to the various men she
encounters on her journey. Like Chariclea and Auristela, who are
initially thought to be goddesses, Fanny creates a kind of veneration
among the hunting squire and his associates: "The Squire and all
the Horsemen were so surprized with her Beauty, that they
immediately fixed both their Eyes and Thoughts solely on her, every
one declaring he had never seen so charming a Creature" (*Joseph
Andrews*, 243). Their amazement, in fact, becomes conventionalized
praise later in the same scene: "Whilst they were on the Road, the
lovely Fanny attracted the Eyes of all; they endeavoured to outvie
one another in Encomiums on her Beauty; which the Reader will
pardon my not relating, as they had not any thing new or uncommon
in them." Although the narrator avoids the clichés, Fanny's beauty
nevertheless brings out the cliché even in the most lustful of men.

Because of her beauty and its effect on the squire, Fanny is
abducted by a group of the squire's men, led by the Captain. Abduction,
of course, is conventional in many forms of adventure fiction, but
the explanation given by the Captain to Parson Adams parallels the
specific conventions of the Heliodoran novel, with an eighteenth-
century twist:

> he had Orders to carry the young Lady with him, whom there was
> great Reason to believe they had stolen from her Parents; for
> notwithstanding her Disguise, her Air, which she could not conceal,
> sufficiently discovered her Birth to be infinitely superiour to theirs.
> (*Joseph Andrews*, 257)

In the Heliodoran tradition, the disguise that the heroine assumes never completely hides her beauty and her nobility; indeed, narrative suspense is often enhanced by the assailant's conviction that the heroine is better born than she pretends to be. In this instance, Fanny is not disguised, but her "Air" of gentility, although masked by her humble status, cannot be disguised. It is worth noting also that Fielding hints at the principal ingredient of several eighteenth-century plots: the abduction of a young girl, like Pamela, by virtuous assailants. By having the captain use a conventional eighteenth-century plot as his excuse to abduct Fanny, Fielding reminds us of the intersection between his story, which is a romance of a different order, and the closer-to-life stories of eighteenth-century romances.

Fanny's "natural Gentility" also plays a role in the recognition scene at the end of the novel. Not only does her beauty cause Mr. Booby to praise her in front of his wife and Lady Booby (causing them to turn to their mirrors to reexamine the mask of their own appearance), but Fanny's turning out to be Pamela's sister also adds an ironic twist to the *Pamela* burlesque with which the novel begins. Instead of unmasking as romance heroines do, Fanny's identity is unmasked for her, and Fanny unmasked, ironically, is Pamela as Pamela should be. By having Fanny momentarily appear to be Joseph's sister, and having the couple vow a "perpetual Celibacy, and to live together all their Days, and indulge in a Platonick Friendship for each other" (*Joseph Andrews*, 335), Fielding—consciously or not—echoes the narrative premise on which the journeys of Theagenes and Chariclea, Periandro and Auristela, and Destiny and Star are based. Instead of lovers disguised as brother and sister, however, these lovers appear to be siblings. Whereas in the Heliodoran tradition the disguise was intended for narrative suspense, here it is intended for narrative surprise. But it is a surprise that creates suspense as well, for without a further unmasking there could be no fulfillment of the implicit promise of a happy ending which the journey, separation, and reunion of the lovers suggest. Fielding thus manipulates the romance pattern so that it effects a double resolution: it brings the hero and heroine to the wished-for happy ending, and it produces a "real" Pamela— an antidote, of sorts, for Richardson's apparently self-serving moralism.

At the very end of the novel Fielding honors these inner qualities of his heroine in a poetic celebration of Fanny's beauty: "Undressing to her was properly discovering, not putting off Ornaments: For as all her Charms were the Gifts of Nature, she could divest herself of none" (*Joseph Andrews*, 343). Indeed, in the subsequent narrative intrusion (which rhetorically resembles the narrator's inability to describe her sensibility, sweetness, or natural gentility in 2.12), Fielding uses the very clichés of romance embellishment:

> How, Reader, shall I give thee an adequate Idea of this lovely young Creature! the Bloom of Roses and Lillies might a little illustrate her Complexion, or their Smell her Sweetness: but to comprehend her entirely, conceive Youth, Health, Bloom, Beauty, Neatness, and Innocence in her Bridal-Bed; conceive all these in their utmost Perfection, and you may place the charming Fanny's Picture before your Eyes. (*Joseph Andrews*, 343)

Whereas Fielding avoided the flower-clichés in the blazon of 2.12, here, after Fanny's identity is revealed, she is accorded the conventional encomia of a romance heroine. By exalting her in this way, Fielding gives his heroine a birthright that far surpasses the relatively small elevation in social status that the unveiling of her real parentage effects.

Like Fanny, Joseph also unwittingly wears a mask through which his natural gentility shines. As a character, however, he presents a slightly different problem of analysis. He is, of course, a male counterpart to Pamela in the early section of the novel: a "Character of Male Chastity" who preserves "his Purity in the midst of so great Temptations" (*Joseph Andrews*, 20). In this role, Joseph writes Pamela-like letters expressing his concern over Lady Booby's lust. But if he is a male version of Richardson's heroine, he is also a modern version of Joseph from Genesis 39, resisting the temptations of Potiphar's wife, and at various points he appears to be a Sancho Panza to Parson Adams's Quixote.

In the middle sections of the novel, however, Joseph bears remarkable similarities to the hero of the Heliodoran novel. Like that hero, Joseph's character is defined almost exclusively as a lover. Just as Theagenes and Chariclea, and Periandro and Auristela are complementary, so Joseph is described in virtually the same terms as Fanny:

> He was of the highest Degree of middle Stature. His Limbs were put together with great Elegance and no less Strength. His Legs and Thighs were formed in the exactest Proportion. His Shoulders were broad and brawny, but yet his Arms hung so easily, that he had all the Symptoms of Strength without the least clumsiness. His Hair was of a nut-brown Colour, and was displayed in wanton Ringlets down his Back. His Forehead was high, his Eyes dark, and as full of Sweetness as of Fire. His Nose a little inclined to the Roman. His Teeth white and even. His Lips full, red, and soft. His Beard was only rough on

his Chin and upper Lip; but his Cheeks, in which his Blood glowed, were overspread with a thick Down. His Countenance had a Tenderness joined with a Sensibility inexpressible. Add to this the most perfect Neatness in his Dress, and an Air, which to those who have not seen many Noblemen, would give an Idea of Nobility. (*Joseph Andrews*, 38)

Not only are Joseph and Fanny genetically similar (nut-brown hair, high foreheads, and noses a little inclining to the Roman), but their internal qualities are well-matched also. Joseph's "Tenderness joined with a Sensibility inexpressible" corresponds to Fanny's incredible sensibility and her "Sweetness beyond either Imitation or Description." Most important, of course, Joseph possesses an "Air" that conveys the "Idea of Nobility."

Joseph's noble air makes him attractive to the various females he encounters during the novel. Betty, the chambermaid at the Towwouse inn, for example, maintains that his white skin suggests he is a gentleman, despite his poverty. Joseph's gentility is later apparent after he has been garbed in his brother-in-law's rich suit of clothes in book 4: "he became it so well, and looked so genteel, that no Person would have doubted its being well adapted to his Quality and Shape" (*Joseph Andrews*, 291). Even more important, Lady Booby recognizes the "Idea of Nobility" in Joseph during her conversation with Mrs. Slipslop in 4.6:

Is he not so genteel that a Prince might without a Blush acknowledge him for his Son. His Behaviour is such that would not shame the best Education. He borrows from his Station a Condescension in every thing to his Superiors, yet unattended by that mean Servility which is called Good Behaviour in such Persons. Every thing he does hath no mark of the base Motive of Fear, but visibly shews some Respect and Gratitude, and carries with it the Persuasion of Love—And then for his Virtues; such Piety to his Parents, such tender Affection to his Sister, such Integrity in his Friendship, such Bravery, such Goodness, that if he had been born a Gentleman, his Wife would have possest the most invaluable Blessing. (*Joseph Andrews*, 295-96)

Her excessive justification of Joseph's status, of course, comically suggests the degree of her passion, but Fielding's close attention to the marks of a hero (piety, integrity, bravery, and goodness) suggests the inner nobility that suitors found in the Heliodoran hero, despite his disguised identity. The irony, of course, is that the very virtues for which Lady Booby admires Joseph make him inaccessible to her.

Parson Adams, like Joseph, is a mixed bag of literary conventions. He roughly parallels Parson Williams in *Pamela* and combines a modern

Don Quixote with a sentimental version of Abraham and Adam. In relation to the two lovers, however, he assumes the roles of guide and spiritual father that Calasiris embodies in the *Aethiopica*. He guides Joseph and Fanny on their journeys both when they are separate and when they are together, and he professes to be their "father," much to the confusion of the innkeepers that the trio encounter. In this respect, his character very much echoes that of Calasiris.

After Calasiris dies in book 7 of the *Aethiopica*, Chariclea laments the loss of her "nurse," "savior," and "father" and sums up his role in the novel: He "conducted us through strange landes, was the stay of our errour, and our guide into our countrie, the knowledge of our parentes, our comfort in adversities, the ease of our ill fortune, the anchore of all our affaires" (*Aethiopica*, 190-91). The parallels with Adams are numerous. He conducts Joseph and Fanny through a land that he suspected was "inhabited only by Jews and Turks" (*Joseph Andrews*, 177). Like Calasiris, he serves as an intermediary in their love. Knowing Joseph's and Fanny's affection for each other from their youth, Adams acts as a go-between in their love, only with "much ado" preventing their marrying at a very young age. When the two lovers are reunited in 2.12 through his agency, Adams sanctions their betrothal, insisting upon the completion of the marriage banns. Just as Calasiris reveals the mystery of Chariclea's identity to her, Parson Adams provides the key, however belatedly, to Joseph's and Fanny's real parentage.

Even more strikingly, Adams serves as an agent of providence in the novel, although the providential design may appear somewhat adventitious. As a priest Calasiris interprets the wisdom of the oracles. Adams, also a priest, derives his wisdom from books, not oracles. Even though he is often out of place in the world, he is, like Calasiris, an agent of providence. When he first meets Joseph at the Towwouse inn, for example, Adams is going to London to sell his sermons to a publisher. When he meets Joseph, he discovers that he has left them at home by accident. He then decides to join Joseph in returning to the country, noting that despite the accident, "it may be intended" for his own good (*Joseph Andrews*, 93). Similarly, after Adams meets Fanny when she is attacked in the woods, he explains that "he doubted not but Providence had sent him to her Deliverance" (*Joseph Andrews*, 139). Moreover, just as Calasiris's involvement with Theagenes and Chariclea brings him back to Memphis, his homeland and the seat of his priesthood, so Parson Adams's association with Joseph and Fanny on the road brings him back to his parish. In fact, Fielding calls attention to his return, in the opening chapter of book 4, by describing it as triumphant and joyous.

If Adams is sage, priest, father figure, and guide, he is also the most fully developed comic figure in the novel. His quixotic simplicity and yet ardent devotion to his office blends into his romance role, very often deflecting attention from it. Like Cervantes' knight, Adams is unable to discern hypocrisy in other people. Even though Adams is ineffectual, his very quixotism advances Fielding's attack on hypocrisy. Unlike Cervantes' knight, however, Adams is not insane; his idealism is not based on a misperception of the real world, but on a belief that people are better than they act. As a result, he naively expects charity from Parson Trulliber in 2.14 because both he and Trulliber are men of the cloth. Similarly, he believes the empty promises of the "Squire" in 2.16. Importantly, both of these actions occur while Adams attempts to care for the needs of his spiritual children, Joseph and Fanny.

In a serious romance such as the *Aethiopica,* we expect a figure like Calasiris to provide the wisdom that the hero and heroine, because of their youth, do not possess. Adams possesses the spiritual wisdom of Calasiris, but not his worldly wisdom. But that Adams should end up accomplishing the same things Calasiris does indicates that Fielding finds hope and redemption in Adams's spiritual wisdom. The romance plot, in essence, redeems the satiric and burlesque episodes in the novel.

Theme and the Heliodoran Novel

It is through Parson Adams that Fielding advances the principal theme of the novel: that Christian benevolence emanates from the integrity of a good-natured heart, even though that goodness often seems out of place in the world. Yet this theme is also a function of the journey and of the accidents that occur to the three principal characters on that journey. In this respect, the Heliodoran tradition again provides a striking parallel to Fielding's novel.

Conventionally, the journey in the Heliodoran novel moves the hero and heroine from a barbaric land to a center of civilization. In the *Aethiopica* the lovers travel from the floods of the Nile Delta, where robbers and pirates reign, southward to Memphis, where the exiled Calasiris dies in his homeland, and finally to Chariclea's homeland, Ethiopia, where barbaric religious customs are changed by virtue of the hero's and heroine's triumphant marriage. In the *Persiles,* as I have noted, the journey begins in northern Europe, where

Christianity, in Cervantes' Counter-Reformation view, had lost the true faith. The destination is to Rome, the center of Roman Catholic civilization and thus the characters' spiritual home. In *Joseph Andrews* the pattern is reversed somewhat in that the general movement is away from London, the center of "civilized" England (where Joseph learns affectations of dress and manners and behaves at church "with less seeming Devotion than formerly"). In its movement back to the country, the novel thematically progresses from a kind of barbarism to a kind of civility.

In one of the first episodes after the novel shifts direction in 1.11—the rescue of Joseph after he is robbed and stripped naked—Fielding outlines his attitude toward the hypocrisies of the civilized world. The coach stops, it is important to note, not because of pure charity, but because one passenger, a lawyer, fears legal recriminations. Even then, however, the coachman only consents to stop when he is offered a mug of beer by a passenger, who sees Joseph's entry into the coach as a chance to show his wit to a female occupant. When Joseph refuses to enter the coach naked, the reaction of the travelers spells out the inherent incivility of the civilized world:

> The two Gentlemen complained they were cold, and could not spare a Rag; the Man of Wit saying, with a laugh, *that Charity began at home*; and the Coachman, who had two great Coats spread under him, refused to lend either, lest they should be made bloody; the Lady's Footman desired to be excused for the same Reason, which the Lady herself, notwithstanding her Abhorrence of a naked Man, approved: and it is more than probable, poor Joseph, who had obstinately adhered to his modest Resolution, must have perished, unless the Postillion, (a Lad who hath been since transported for robbing a Hen-roost) had voluntarily stript off a great Coat, his only Garment, at the same time swearing a great Oath, (for which he was rebuked by the Passengers) "that he would rather ride in his Shirt all his Life, than suffer a Fellow-Creature to lie in so miserable a Condition." (*Joseph Andrews*, 53)

The passengers depicted here are concerned with preserving the appearances of civilized behavior. Their fastidiousness about their clothing, the man of wit's espousing the cliché about charity's beginning at home, and the revulsion of the passengers at the postilion's oath all attest to it. Only the postilion, whose later transportation for robbery places him outside the pale of the civilized world, possesses the kind of charity that a Christian civilization should display.

The distinction between the greed of the well-to-do and the innate goodness of the simple continues throughout the journey. The wealthy Parson Trulliber, a man who had "charity" always in his mouth though he never gave a farthing, refuses Parson Adams's plea for a loan. Adams's, Joseph's, and Fanny's financial distresses are relieved by a poor peddler who offers Adams his only sixpence. At the following inn, where Adams is enjoined to spend more than his means by the empty promises of an apparent gentleman, a kindly innkeeper forgoes the tab, causing Adams to reflect on the barbarity of the land through which he was traveling: "he was glad to find some Christians left in the Kingdom; for that he almost began to suspect that he was sojourning in a Country inhabited only by Jews and Turks" (*Joseph Andrews*, 177). The area between the City and the Country thus becomes a metaphorical wasteland, a place of barbarism. The really charitable seem out of place: the peddler, the postilion, the innkeeper of 3.16 and 17 (the last of whom failed to secure a position in the Admiralty), and Wilson (who placed himself in a virtual exile because of his struggles in the civilized world). Civilized people, or those who affect to be such, display barbarism characterized by their selfishness and hypocrisy.

Conclusion

Although all of the parallels I have drawn between the Heliodoran novel and *Joseph Andrews* could easily be attributed to the vast pool of romance literature available to the author, the Heliodoran novel illuminates the kind of controlled design that Fielding seems to intend. It is a design that does not simply parody romance conventions but integrates romance into a narrative that presents the contingencies of history.

Joseph, Fanny, and Adams have their feet in both romance and history. On the one hand, they are inferior in rank and manners and participate in the comically realistic world which, because of their unworldly naiveté, often makes them the butt of humor. At the same time, however, they are idealized characters. Joseph and Fanny, in spite of their low station, possess an inner nobility; Adams, in spite of his quixotic myopia, becomes an agent of providence. Their ideal qualities—their romance qualities, in fact—elevate them above the status they would have in a merely parodic work. Indeed, when we consider a work like *Jonathan Wild,* where Fielding uses romance conventions to reduce a rogue history to absurdity, we can see fairly clearly the difference between Fielding's parodic and nonparodic use of romance conventions.

In *Jonathan Wild* vestiges of the Heliodoran pattern appear in the subplot concerning the Heartfrees. Wild, like so many rivals in the heroic novels, pretends a friendship to Heartfree because he is enamored of Heartfree's wife. Because of Wild's plotting, she is abducted and plagued by the kind of adventures that occur in the Heliodoran novel: attempted rapes, subsequent abductions by more villainous figures, a shipwreck, and a roundabout journey before she is reunited with her husband. Like the heroines of the Heliodoran novel, she protects her husband's jewels amidst all her trials, and these jewels suggest, as they do in the *Persiles,* both her fortune and her chastity. Heartfree, for his part, plays the role of a romance hero, if not in his heroism, at least in his conventional response to the events that befall the couple. After his wife's disappearance, he entertains doubts of her fidelity and, like a conventional romance hero, laments the cruelty of fortune. When Mrs. Heartfree delivers the lengthy recital of her adventures, he experiences conventionally passionate upheavals at the very mention of attacks on her virtue. Fielding constructs the subplot, in short, so that it follows the conventional formula of romance and so that it stresses the conclusion that Mrs. Heartfree makes at the end of her recital: "THAT PROVIDENCE WILL SOONER OR LATER PROCURE THE FELICITY OF THE VIRTUOUS AND THE INNOCENT."[11]

Although Fielding emphasizes the internal qualities of the Heartfrees in this romance subplot, as he does in *Joseph Andrews,* his overall use of romance elements does not resolve the plot as it does in his other novels. Instead, it provides a patently implausible view of a world quite different from Wild's. The romance conventions correct the meaning of Wild's heroically criminal "greatness," but the norm implied is consciously set up as silly by the ironic narrator. In *Joseph Andrews*—as in *Tom Jones* and *Amelia*—the romance norm is not comic relief, nor is it patently implausible. It is, rather, the supporting structure of the novel. Indeed, as Fielding builds more complex plots, the relationship between the internal structure of romance and the external appearance of his novels becomes less evident, but the pattern I have defined as the Heliodoran novel's is still evident and will explain how the romance conventions support an otherwise causal similar plot.

5

The Romance Infrastructure of *Tom Jones*

Like *Joseph Andrews, Tom Jones* begins with every appearance of being a history. Fielding's title for book 1 establishes the pattern: "Containing as much of the Birth of the Foundling as is necessary or proper to acquaint the Reader with in the Beginning of this History." By stressing "beginning" and the birth of the title character here, and by mentioning some passage of time in each of the headings for the remaining seventeen books, Fielding establishes at least a surface appearance of chronological narration. Indeed, if we consider the usual tripartite division of the novel (six books in Somerset, six on the road, and six in London), there is a superficial appearance of space as well as time.

Tom Jones, however, is a novel that cannot be appreciated at first glance—no matter how careful that first glance is. It takes on a vastly different appearance when the reader finishes it and learns of Bridget Allworthy's "Summer" love and of Thomas Blifil's perfidy throughout. What appears on first reading to be an empirical selection of facts, presented by a narrator who dwells on certain scenes and passes over others, turns out to be a very adept suppression of clues. Although our recognition of these clues does not alter the material evidence of Tom's sexual imprudence, and although the information about his birth does not make him any less a bastard, the resolution of the novel confirms a sense most readers have about the fittingness of a romance ending for Tom's history. This fittingness, however, does not result from our sense of Jones as a conventional romance hero and Sophia as his conventional counterpart. Indeed, the surface pattern of the novel moves us away from romance conventionality.

The fittingness results, rather, from our belief in Tom's goodness despite his appearance of being a rogue. The romance pattern that emerges when the novel is finished serves as a kind of infrastructure by which Fielding unifies and directs the causal-similar history of Tom's antiromance behavior.[1]

As in *Joseph Andrews,* the romance structure of *Tom Jones* roughly parallels the action of the Heliodoran novel. In the first six books of the novel—the Somerset section—we learn of Tom's and Sophia's love, which develops in spite of the mystery surrounding the hero's identity and in spite of the objections of the heroine's father. Like the conventionally tyrannical parent of sentimental and romance literature, Squire Western proposes a suitor for Sophia who becomes the hero's principal rival. In the middle six books—the "road" section—we have a separation of the lovers that eventually becomes a mutual quest. In the last six books—the London section—we have the hero's and heroine's arrival at a center of civilization. We are introduced to new complications: a series of dilemmas that make their marriage seem impossible. After the hero's identity is finally revealed, there is a reconciliation and marriage.

Whereas in *Joseph Andrews* the romance plot virtually breaks away from the kind of history that begins the novel, and sets up a journey analogous to that in the Heliodoran tradition, in *Tom Jones* the romance structure provides a retrospective unity to the novel that forces us to reevaluate the causal progression of events. Even though the novel takes on the appearance of history from the very start, it becomes clear by the ending that the causal-similar accidents are as contrived as those in any providentially ordered romance. In shaping the novel as he does, Fielding effects a synthesis between romance and history that is aesthetically similar to the synthesis effected by the Heliodoran novelists.

Romance and the Ending of Tom Jones

To understand how this infrastructure works, let us begin at the end, for it is not until we finish the novel that we recognize how carefully unified it is.

In the last three books of the novel, Fielding creates a kind of suspense that is quite similar to the third phase of the Heliodoran novel, when the hero and heroine face seemingly insurmountable obstacles. Tom and Sophia, each having arrived in London, are brought into close proximity, but are not reunited. Lady Bellaston—like Thomyris in the *Cyrus,* Hipólita in the *Persiles,* and Arsace in the

Aethiopica—has created havoc for both the hero and the heroine. She has urged Lord Fellamar to rape Sophia, and when that failed, gave Tom's proposal letter to Mrs. Western, who shows it to Sophia, as Lady Bellaston intended. While Lady Bellaston's plot to avenge herself upon Tom is in motion, the hero is thrown in jail for allegedly assaulting Mr. Fitzpatrick, who assumed Tom was his rival with Harriet Fitzpatrick. Unlike the Heliodoran novel, however, where divine providence goes hand in hand with narrative suspense, Tom himself is the cause of his own troubles—a fact that suspends our rhetorical expectations of a romance pattern.[2] Later, when Tom supposes that Mrs. Waters is his mother, the narrative tension reaches a higher pitch and creates complications that would be difficult to resolve even in the most improbable of romances.

Fielding comments on the suspense he has manipulated in the prefatory chapter to book 17: "When a Comic Writer hath made his principal Characters as happy as he can; or when a Tragic Writer hath brought them to the highest Pitch of human Misery, they both conclude their Business to be done, and that their Work is come to a Period" (*Tom Jones*, 875). Like many of Fielding's narrative intrusions, this one emphasizes our roles as discerning readers. We must respond not only to the narrative suspense, but also to the author's choric manipulation of suspense.

This choric suspense, interestingly enough, points out the intersection between romance and history in the novel. Noting the difficulty of bringing his "Favourites out of their present Anguish" and landing them "at last on the Shore of Happiness," Fielding reaffirms the causal-similar pose he has adopted throughout the novel:

> This I faithfully promise, that notwithstanding any Affection which we may be supposed to have for this Rogue, whom we have unfortunately made our Heroe, we will lend him none of that supernatural Assistance with which we are entrusted, upon Condition that we use it only on very important Occasions. If he doth not therefore find some natural Means of fairly extricating himself from all his Distresses, we will do no Violence to the Truth and Dignity of History for his Sake; for we had rather relate that he was hanged at Tyburn (which may very probably be the Case) than forfeit our Integrity, or shock the Faith of our Reader. (*Tom Jones*, 875-76)

By disavowing any supernatural assistance and by defending the truth and dignity of history, Fielding overtly denies any kind of romance control over history. Nevertheless, the intrusive commentary itself prepares the reader for a romance conclusion that arises out of the natural or causal-similar progression of events. If we took the narrator seriously here, the kind of ending we should expect would be quite different from the ending we get. We should expect Jones to be hanged and Sophia to marry "either Blifil, or my Lord, or some Body else" (*Tom Jones*, 875). Yet we do not completely believe the narrator, or to be more precise, we have been programmed throughout to accept a different "Faith" from that prompted by causal similitude. Although the means by which Jones is extricated are "natural," and although Fielding invokes no "supernatural Assistance," the medley of events that reveals Tom's identity and punishes Blifil is contrived. That very contrivance, in fact, redefines the "Truth and Dignity of History."

Looking back on the plot from the vantage point of the ending, we can see that Fielding has programmed us to look for truth beneath the surface of events. Indeed, he has trained us, by virtue of the discrimination his narrator makes between good- and ill-natured readers, to see truth from two quite different perspectives. The first is an antiromance, antisentimental, empirical view; it prompts us to expect a rogue history that could as easily end with a hanging as a redemption. The second is a romance, sentimental, and intuitive view; it depends to a large degree on the narrator's good-natured judgments and on our belief in something akin to poetic justice.[3] These two vantage points are not diametrically opposed. Tom is still a bastard at the end of the novel; his infidelity to Sophia threatens to keep them apart even after Tom's parentage is unveiled and his good-natured benevolence demonstrated. Fielding manages, however, to reconcile the providential guidance of romance with the causality of history.

Books 13-18: Phases Three and Four

The final six books of *Tom Jones* not only make us see the novel's implicit foundation, but they also parallel events in phases three and four of the Heliodoran novel. By looking at these phases before we examine the first two phases, we shall see how carefully Fielding has suppressed romance clues throughout the novel. In the last six books the lovers arrive at London, where they undergo complications that make their marriage seem impossible. The journey that led them there, of course, is only partially conventional. Sophia consciously pursues Jones to Upton, and he consciously pursues her after that, but they do not journey together—a deviation from the pattern of the Heliodoran novel. Nevertheless, the suspense Fielding creates when the lovers are reunited at Lady Bellaston's in 13.11 parallels the suspense of the Heliodoran novel and gives us a glimpse of a possible romance ending. Their reunion is a complex mixture of sentimental cliché, romance convention, and dramatic irony that makes one aware of the mixture of romance and antiromance circumstances that contribute toward it.

In the Heliodoran novel the various reunions of the lovers are punctuated by embellished descriptions of their joy and surprise and by lengthy recitals of their adventures while apart. Fielding provides a rhetorical embellishment in describing Tom's and Sophia's meeting, but ironically the embellishment emphasizes their silence, not their overt expression of joy:

> To paint the Looks or Thoughts of either of these Lovers is beyond my Power. As their Sensations, from their mutual Silence, may be judged to have been too big for their own Utterance, it cannot be supposed, that I should be able to express them: And the Misfortune is, that few of my Readers have been enough in Love, to feel by their own Hearts what past at this Time in theirs. (*Tom Jones*, 730-31)

In a more conventional romance (or in a more sentimental romance, for that matter), the lovers' silence most likely would be supplanted by lengthy rhetorical outbursts. Fielding's silence heightens both the irony and the suspense. Even though Tom's and Sophia's meeting renews our hopes for a romance ending, part of what passed in Tom's heart undoubtedly is anxiety about how to explain his presence at Lady Bellaston's.

Curiously, the dramatic irony of the scene (our knowledge of Tom's affair with Lady Bellaston and Sophia's ignorance of it) leads to a second level of irony that resembles the conventional dilemma in various Heliodoran novels. Tom, mindful of Sophia's near discovery of him at Upton, professes a romance fidelity to the heroine:

> Though I despaired of possessing you, nay, almost of ever seeing you more, I doated still on your charming Idea, and could *seriously* love no other Woman: But if my Heart had not been engaged, she, into whose Company I accidentally fell at that cursed Place, was not the Object of serious Love. (*Tom Jones*, 732)

Assuming that Sophia is angered at his bedding Mrs. Waters, Tom does not deny his antiromance behavior but, instead, professes a higher love. Sophia, however, is not angered at Tom's bedding Mrs. Waters, but at the false intelligence she has received from Partridge that he has traduced her name in public. Although guilty of crimes no romance hero could be, Tom is nevertheless, like Cyrus, the victim of false rumors.[4] When the mistake is cleared up and the lovers are reconciled, the romance plot is set back on track. They even tell officious lies to Lady Bellaston, as Heliodoran novel lovers do when they attempt to disguise the fact that they are lovers.

The irony of Tom's and Sophia's meeting with Lady Bellaston prevents our full engagement in the romance potential of the scene, of course. Tom lies not only to Lady Bellaston, but also to Sophia. Nevertheless, the hero's and heroine's reunion, like the arrival of the Heliodoran-novel hero and heroine at their destination, changes the focus of the narrative. Instead of a loose string of accidents occurring over the course of a journey, the knots of complication, like the third phase of the Heliodoran novel, are clustered in one central locale. Sophia is plagued by parental tyranny in the form of both Squire Western and his sister. Blifil, Tom's primary rival, reappears and is championed by Allworthy, a kind of parental impediment to Tom's hopes. Lady Bellaston, like Hipólita in the *Persiles* and Arsace in the *Aethiopica,* attempts to ruin Sophia by arranging for Lord Fellamar to rape the heroine. Tom, after getting free of Lady Bellaston, is pursued by Arabella Hunt and Mrs. Fitzpatrick. Although he resists both like a dutiful romance hero, his conversation with the latter causes his duel with Fitzpatrick, which precipitates Tom's imprisonment.

As befits a novel guided by causal similitude, most of the complications in this phase are directly or indirectly caused by the hero. It is worth noting, however, that the events leading Tom to the brink of misery are based on false rumor. Fitzpatrick wrongly supposes that Tom was having an affair with his wife; Tom's proposal letter to Lady Bellaston is a ruse; and both Partridge and Tom wrongly suppose that Mrs. Waters is Tom's mother. Add to these Blifil's plot with Lawyer Dowling to buy witnesses against Tom, and Allworthy's blind conviction that Tom is a hopeless reprobate, and we have a Gordian knot of complications that makes one long for the kind of intervention of truth possible only in romance.

In the Heliodoran novel, the truth about the hero's or heroine's identity is the central truth that restores order to the novel. In *Tom Jones* the truth about Tom's parentage prepares the way for the resolution of the novel, but the happy ending depends on the truth of Tom's inner nobility being unveiled. The evidence Mrs. Miller provides about Tom's generosity to her cousin and her family, as well as the investigation she and Partridge undertake about the suborned witnesses against Tom, removes the appearance of villainy that Tom has in Allworthy's eyes. The revelation of Tom's parentage thus is virtually a symbolic gesture: it signals a romance current in the plot that runs deeper than romance appearances. Tom, unmasked of his roguery, is a good-natured hero, and Blifil, unmasked of his cloying moralism, is a worse villain than we supposed.

Although the revelation of Tom's identity and his vindication in Allworthy's eyes confirm what sympathetic readers have long desired for the hero, the final resolution of the novel depends on one final test: Tom's ability to convince Sophia that he is worthy of her. In the Heliodoran novel—indeed, in any romance—the reconciliation of the lovers would be inevitable. Tom can explain that his proposal to Lady Bellaston was a ruse. He can even honestly profess a sincere repentance. Yet the truth of his actions—the truth of his identity in the causal-similar episodes of the novel—threatens to leave the novel unresolved.

The resolution demands not the triumph of ideal truth, but an acceptance of human imperfection. "Sincere repentance," Sophia tells the hero, "will obtain the Pardon of a Sinner, but it is from one who is a perfect Judge of that Sincerity. A human Mind may be imposed on; nor is there any infallible Method to prevent it" (*Tom Jones*, 972). Sophia's insistence on a period of time during which Tom can demonstrate his constancy threatens to reopen the novel with another journey, perhaps a more conventionally romanesque one. Yet when the lovers agree on this betrothal pact, a parental complication emerges, ironically like that which opens the Heliodoran novel. Squire Western, like the conventionally tyrannical father, insists on Sophia's marrying according to his dictates. In this case, however, the conventionality is comically introduced and happily thwarted. Western's conventional tyranny ironically becomes a realistic force that drives the plot to a romance conclusion.

The final phase—the marriage—takes place without ostentatious ceremony, but not without hints at a romance triumph. As in many of the Heliodoran novels, the hero's and heroine's marriage takes place simultaneously with that of subordinate characters. Tom and Sophia marry at the same time the two Nightingale cousins marry the women their fathers initially objected to. Sophia's beauty, however, outshines that of both other brides. To the two Nightingales, she is like a "Queen receiving Homage, or rather like a superiour Being receiving Adoration from all around her" (Tom Jones, 978). Like Chariclea when she assumes the role as priestess at the end of the *Aethiopica,* Sophia approaches the divine here, even though the narrator is cautious to point out that it was "an Adoration which they gave, not which she expected."

The novel ends, or rather comes close to an ending, with a rhetorical flourish that stresses romance fulfillment:

Thus, Reader, we have at length brought our History to a Conclusion,
in which, to our great Pleasure, tho' contrary perhaps to thy
Expectation, Mr. Jones appears to be the happiest of all human Kind:
For what Happiness this World affords equal to the Possession of such
a Woman as Sophia, I sincerely own I have never yet discovered.
(*Tom Jones*, 979)

Having at last landed the hero and heroine on the shore of happiness,
Fielding extends the history two or three pages beyond this conclusion.
In part, this extension gives a causal-similar accounting of what
fortunes are settled on which characters, but the intent is clearly
to contrast the mere tying-up of matters for other characters and
the exultation over Tom's and Sophia's happiness.

Books 1-6: Phase One

When we consider the first twelve books of *Tom Jones* in light
of the last six, it becomes clear that, despite the intricate ways Fielding
diverts our attention from clues relating to Tom's birth, our sense
of the rightness of the ending depends on the dual role Tom plays
throughout the plot. In his antiromance role, Tom is something like
a *pícaro:* a hungry young man whose aimless journey, like his lifestyle,
is episodic.[5] In his romance role, Tom is a conventional hero whose
adventures proceed directly from his love for Sophia. The pattern
of these romance adventures is diffused by his antiromance actions,
but Fielding's presentation of Tom and Sophia prompts us to see a
romance design in the peripatetics of the plot.

In the first six books of the novel, Tom's love for Sophia develops
in many ways like the love in the Heliodoran novel. Not unlike
Theagenes in the court of Caricles, or Artamène in the court of
Cyaxare, Tom becomes a champion of the heroine's father: first when
he attempts to rescue Sophia's little bird "Tommy," and later when
he rescues Sophia from an unruly horse. The latter action awakens
Sophia's love for Tom and sufficiently raises Squire Western's esteem
for the hero so that he invites Tom to stay at his estate, thus
inadvertently encouraging the hero's and heroine's love.

In a novel where sentimental heroism prevails, it is natural that
Tom's and Sophia's love should first display itself in terms of a
sentimental ritual. In 4.5, shortly after Sophia's return to Somerset
from her aunt's, the hero and heroine meet alone for the first time
and Tom, in a reticent and serious manner, "began . . . to acquaint
her, that he had a Favour to ask of her, which he hoped her Goodness
would comply with" (*Tom Jones*, 167). Although the "Favour" is

nothing more than to ask her to intercede with her father on Black George's behalf, Fielding pauses to exploit the sentimental and romance potential of the scene:

> Though neither the young Man's Behaviour, nor indeed his Manner of opening this Business, were such as could give her any just Cause of suspecting he intended to make Love to her; yet, whether Nature whispered something into her Ear, or from what Cause it arose I will not determine, certain it is, some Idea of that Kind must have intruded itself; for her Colour forsook her Cheeks, her Limbs trembled, and her Tongue would have faultered, had Tom stopped for an Answer. (*Tom Jones*, 167)

What Fielding depicts here is a sentimental, romance psychology of love: Sophia's heart is sensitive to Tom's unspoken words, because of his backward manner and his very seriousness.

When Sophia asks a reciprocal "Favour" from Jones, he exclaims in the manner of a sentimentalized knight whose code of chivalry is philosophical benevolence:

> A Favour, Madam . . . if you knew the Pleasure you have given me in the Hopes of receiving a Command from you, you would think by mentioning it you did confer the greatest Favour on me; for by this dear Hand I would sacrifice my Life to oblige you. (*Tom Jones*, 168)

Tom then snatches her hand and "eagerly" kisses it, an action motivated by his unselfish heart and his willingness to serve as her champion.

Sophia responds to Jones's speech and courtesy more directly in the manner of an eighteenth-century sentimental heroine:

> The Blood, which before had forsaken her Cheeks, now made her sufficient Amends, by rushing all over her Face and Neck with such Violence, that they became all of a scarlet Colour. She first felt a Sensation to which she had been before a Stranger, and which, when she had Leisure to reflect on it, began to acquaint her with some Secrets, which the Reader, if he doth not already guess them, will know in Time. (*Tom Jones*, 168)

The secrets, of course, are the sensations of love taken in by her heart. The emphasis on "sensations" and the narrator's candid reticence about identifying them are typical of the sentimental love depicted in a variety of plays and novels of the period. But they also emphasize Fielding's conscious effort, at this stage of the novel, to plant the suggestions of a romance pattern that Tom's antisentimental and antiromance relationship with Molly Seagrim will later complicate.

Although Sophia's love is more sentimental than romanesque,

the way it develops bears interesting parallels to the love in the Heliodoran novel. Just as Chariclea was a "scorner" of love, Sophia is a "Stranger" to these feelings. She loses her heart to Jones even before she "suspected it was in Danger" (*Tom Jones*, 167). Just as Chariclea endures a lovesickness because of her growing affection for Theagenes, so the first movements of love in Sophia's heart manifest themselves in physical sensations. Whereas Chariclea's love malady could be "cured" by Calasiris's bringing the lovers together, Sophia's is not so easily cured. After her father jokes about Molly Seagrim's pregnancy at table (much to the embarrassment of the hero), Sophia is consciously affected both by love and by a sense of decorum: "Her Heart now, at once, discovered the great Secret to her, which it had been so long disclosing by little and little; and she found herself highly interested in this Matter" (*Tom Jones*, 190). Ironically, of course, Sophia's love for Jones becomes clear to her after he violates the conventional behavior of a hero. Once she is aware of her feelings, she endures a sleepless night (4.12), resulting both from her thoughts of Tom's indiscretion and from her growing love. Later, the narrator analyzes the heroine's feelings in terms of a complex physical ailment:

> The Reader will be pleased to recollect, that a secret Affection for Mr. Jones had insensibly stolen into the Bosom of this young Lady. That it had grown there to a pretty great Height before she had discovered it. When she first began to perceive its Symptoms, the Sensations were so great and pleasing, that she had not Resolution sufficient to check or repel them; and thus she went on cherishing a Passion of which she never once considered the Consequences. (*Tom Jones*, 197-98)

Unlike the Heliodoran heroine, whose love malady reveals her love to a stranger, Sophia's is directed inward—revealing her love to herself. Indeed, Sophia's malady manifests the central conflict of the novel: her awareness of her "romance" love for Jones but her desire to dispel it because of her knowledge of Jones's antiromance behavior. It is curious to note that Tom's affair with Molly Seagrim serves as a "nauseous Physic" that "for the Time expelled her Distemper" (*Tom Jones*, 198). In spite of this physic, however, the disease is not entirely eradicated. When she is once again face-to-face with Jones, the distemper relapses: "all the former Symptoms returned, and from that Time cold and hot fits alternately seized her Heart" (*Tom Jones*, 199).

Unlike the first phase of the Heliodoran novel, in which the principal obstacle to the hero's and heroine's marriage is the objection of a parent, in *Tom Jones* Fielding introduces the Molly Seagrim affair to demonstrate how much Tom is, in Sophia's words, "no-body's Enemy but his own" (*Tom Jones*, 165). It is significant that the information about Molly is not reported until Tom has become sensibly affected by Sophia. Such an ordering forces the reader to accept Tom's love for Sophia as romance wish fulfillment, not as the kind of opportunism that might suggest itself, were the events reported as they happened. Indeed, Fielding seems to intend a sharp contrast between Sophia and Molly in order to point out two potential directions in the plot, both of which eventually happen: a romance story in which Tom's ideal love for Sophia undergoes many of the obstacles we find in the Heliodoran tradition, and an episodic story of Tom's sexual hunger. Fielding makes these two threads of the plot clear by the different ways he introduces Sophia and Molly.

Sophia is introduced in 4.2 with a rhetorical flourish much like the conventional, embellished descriptions of heroines in the Heliodoran novel. Like Fanny in *Joseph Andrews*, Sophia combines nature and art, but in his blazon of Sophia, Fielding takes the poetic clichés more seriously. Her hair, for instance, was "curled so gracefully . . . that few could believe it to be her own" (*Tom Jones*, 156). Her eyebrows were "full, even, and arched beyond the Power of Art to imitate." Her teeth were "two Rows of Ivory;" her lips "had more of the Lily than of the Rose, but when Exercise, or Modesty, encreased her natural Colour, no Vermilion could equal it" (*Tom Jones*, 157). Her neck exceeded the beauty of Venus de Medici and the whiteness of lilies, ivory, or alabaster. Her bosom shined beyond "the purest Brightness of Parian Marble" (*Tom Jones*, 157).

These clichés establish Sophia as an idealized figure, perfectly appropriate for the romance thread of the novel. Later in book 4, however, Fielding's description of Molly distinctly contrasts with this idealized view of the heroine:

> though Molly was . . . generally thought to be a very fine Girl, and in reality she was so, yet her Beauty was not of the most amiable Kind. It had indeed very little of the Feminine in it, and would have become a Man at least as well as a Woman; for to say the Truth, Youth and florid Health had a very considerable Share in the Composition. (*Tom Jones*, 174-75)

Unlike Sophia, whose "Sweetness" diffuses a "Glory over her Countenance, which no Regularity of Features can give," Molly is "tall and robust" in stature and "bold and forward" in personality. Tom initially reacts to Molly's forwardness with a backwardness that is analogous to his reticence toward Sophia. Ultimately, however, it prompts him to a different manner of "heroic" behavior:

So little had she of Modesty, that Jones had more Regard for her Virtue than she herself. And as most probably she liked Tom as well as he liked her, so when she perceived his Backwardness, she herself grew proportionately forward; and when she saw he had entirely deserted [her] House, she found Means of throwing herself in his Way, and behaved in such a Manner, that the Youth must have had very much, or very little of the Hero, if her Endeavours had proved unsuccessful. In a Word, she soon triumphed over all the virtuous Resolutions of Jones: For though she behaved at last with all decent Reluctance, yet I rather chuse to attribute the Triumph to her: Since in Fact, it was her Design which succeeded. (*Tom Jones*, 175)

Tom's having very much of the hero implies the kind of chaste love that heroes such as Cyrus and Oroondates possess. Fielding, indeed, alludes to such a quality in Tom when Tom visits Mrs. Fitzpatrick in 16.9.[6] Having very little of the hero, curiously enough, implies the kind of lusty, virile, splendidly wicked role that has since become almost the only thing many readers remember about *Tom Jones*.[7] The paradoxical alternatives of being very much or very little of the hero exactly define the dilemma that faces Tom in this first phase of the novel.

In the prefatory chapter to the sixth book of the novel—the last of this first phase—Fielding offers a philosophical discourse on two notions of love that arise from Tom's dilemma. The essay is cast as a refutation of ill-natured philosophers who argue that there is no such passion as Love "in the human Breast" and argue, rather, that this passion is hunger: "the Desire of satisfying a voracious Appetite with a certain Quantity of delicate white human Flesh" (*Tom Jones*, 270). The narrator counters this definition of love by asserting that love is "a kind and benevolent Disposition, which is gratified by contributing to the Happiness of others." The pleasures arising from "pure Love" may be "heightened and sweetened by the Assistance of amorous Desires," but the pleasures can exist without those desires and are not destroyed by them.

Fielding clinches the argument by comparing the ill natured reader, who does not understand his definition of benevolent love, to Locke's celebrated blind man, who confuses colors with sound:

To treat of the Effects of Love to you, must be as absurd as to discourse on Colours to a Man born blind; since possibly your Idea of Love may be as absurd as that which we are told such blind Man once entertained of the Colour Scarlet: that Colour seemed to him to be very much like the Sound of a Trumpet; and Love probably may, in your Opinion, very greatly resemble a Dish of Soup, of a Sir-loin of Roast beef. (*Tom Jones*, 271-72)

Tom's romance love for the idealized, sentimentalized heroine clearly suggests the position of the benevolent philosophers, but his actions with Molly in the rutting episode, and later with Mrs. Waters and Lady Bellaston, also suggest that he is guided as much by Hunger as by Love.[8] What is curious is the emphasis Fielding's analogy places on our faculty of understanding benevolent love. Ill-natured readers have an impairment of their sensibility—their moral sense—which prevents them from distinguishing love from hunger, just as blindness prevents the man from distinguishing sound from color.[9] And just as we are forced to understand the ill-natured philosophers' position about benevolent love, we are forced to accept the antiromance events in the novel, even though what sustains the plot are the romance events. The opposition of the two kinds of love suggests that our task as readers is to see and understand a romance pattern that is temporarily thwarted by antiromance complications.

Tom's benevolent love for Sophia is often vented by means of hyperbole, casting him as a romance hero, if not by his actions at least by his language. While he is drunk with wine and exhilaration at the news of Allworthy's recovery, Tom breaks forth into an "Ejaculation" that would befit Oroondates or any other hero besotted with romance love:

> O Sophia, would Heaven give thee to my Arms, how blest would be my Condition! Curst be that Fortune which sets a Distance between us. Was I but possessed of thee, one only Suit of Rags thy whole Estate, is there a Man on Earth whom I would envy! How contemptible would the brightest Circassian Beauty, drest in all the Jewels of the Indies, appear to my Eyes! But why do I mention another Woman? could I think my Eyes capable of looking at any other with Tenderness, these Hands should tear them from my Head. No, my Sophia, if cruel Fortune separates us for ever, my Soul shall doat on thee alone. The chastest Constancy I will preserve to thy Image. Though I should never have Possession of thy charming Person, still shalt thou alone have Possession of my Thoughts, my Love, my Soul. Oh! my fond Heart is so wrapt in that tender Bosom, that the brightest Beauties would for me have no Charms, nor would a Hermit be colder in their Embraces. Sophia, Sophia alone shall be mine. What Raptures are in that Name! I will engrave it on every Tree. (*Tom Jones*, 256)

Tom's apostrophe runs a gamut of romance clichés: a prayer to providence and a lament on fortune in the first two sentences, a rhetorical question punctuated by an exclamation in the third, and a litotical comparison in the fourth. In the fifth, sixth, and seventh sentences Tom brings himself out of romance comparisons only to launch forth again in a hyperbolic and Platonic avowal of constancy in sentences eight and nine. These are followed by another litotical comparison, an exclamation that Sophia will be his despite the distance between them in social status, a rapturous exclamation on her name, and a decision (like a conventional pastoral lover) to carve her name, hyperbolically, on every tree.

The rhetoric of the passage is undercut by Tom's finding not Sophia at the end of his ejaculation, but Molly. Molly's presence leads him from an intoxication with romance rhetoric to lust. Their rutting leads to a confrontation with Thwackum and Blifil, which plays no small part in Tom's later expulsion from Allworthy's estate. The confrontation also sets up a further alliance between Tom and Squire Western that eventually leads to Tom's direct profession of his love for Sophia.

Two other related events bring this first phase of the novel to a conclusion similar to that in the Heliodoran novel. First, Western plays the role of a tyrannical father and arranges for Sophia to marry the gentleman most suitable for his property and most odious to his daughter's taste: Thomas Blifil. This event leads to a near battle between Jones and Western, upon the latter's discovery of Tom's and Sophia's affection. Not unlike Justinian's encounter with Isabelle's father in the *Ibrahim,* the hero resists a fight with the heroine's father. Western's discovery of Tom's love necessitates the hero's departure from the heroine and sets up the journey in the middle six books of the novel.

Second, in spite of Western's objection to Tom's and Sophia's marriage, the lovers exchange marital vows—after a fashion, at least. In 6.9 Sophia gives Tom an indirect promise that she will not marry Blifil: "Be assured I never will give him what is in my Power to with-hold from him" (*Tom Jones*, 299). Later, after Tom's dismissal from Allworthy's, Sophia sends a letter to Jones that is as much of a betrothal as causal similitude in this novel allows:

> Sir,
> "It is impossible to express what I have felt since I saw you. Your submitting, on my Account, to such cruel Insults from my Father, lays me under an Obligation I shall ever own. As you know his Temper, I beg you will, for my Sake, avoid him. I wish I had any Comfort to send you; but believe this, that nothing but the last Violence shall ever give my Hand or Heart where you would be sorry to see them bestowed." (*Tom Jones*, 315)

This promise is not the kind of ritual betrothal scene we find in the *Aethiopica* or the *Persiles,* nor is it contingent upon the kind of promise Mandane extracts from Artamène—that he will find some means of resurrecting his real identity. Nevertheless, Sophia's letter gives Tom "some little Glimpse of Hope from her Constancy, of some favourable Accident hereafter" (*Tom Jones*, 315).

Books 7-12: Phase Two

The mixture of Tom's romance love and antiromance hunger in the first six books of the novel prepares us for a similar mixture of romance and antiromance conventions in the middle six books. Tom's forced departure, Black George's appropriation of the banknotes Allworthy gave the hero, and the rumors that Tom was sent away penniless and naked from his reputed father's house suggest that Tom's journey is like the *pícaro's*. Indeed, the narrator seems to suggest as much in his commentary on the hero's plight: "What Course of Life to pursue, or what Business to apply himself . . . was all a Melancholy Void. Every Profession, and every Trade, required Length of Time, and what was worse, Money" (*Tom Jones*, 331).

The *pícaro's* journey, like Tom's, is launched by hunger and poverty, yet Tom's is cast in something of an antipicaresque manner after his guide loses the way to Bristol. In 7.11 Tom joins up with a troop of soldiers who are marching against the Jacobites:

> Jones had some Heroic Ingredients in his Composition, and was a hearty Well-wisher to the glorious Cause of Liberty, and of the Protestant Religion. It is no wonder, therefore, that in Circumstances which would have warranted a much more romantick and wild Undertaking, it should occur to him to serve as a Volunteer in this Expedition. (*Tom Jones*, 368)

Like Justinian, who goes off to war after he is separated from Isabelle, Tom follows the path of heroic fortune. Indeed, his first action with the soldiers is a confrontation with Northerton, who has maligned Sophia in a toast. Fielding uses the episode to define Tom's heroic potential, even though that potential is qualified by naiveté:

> The Tenderness of Lovers can ill brook the least jesting with the Names of their Mistresses. However, Jones, tho' he had enough of the Lover and of the Heroe too in his Disposition, did not resent these Slanders as hastily as, perhaps, he ought to have done. To say the Truth, having seen but little of this Kind of Wit, he did not readily understand it, and for a long Time imagined Mr. Northerton had really mistaken his Charmer for some other. (*Tom Jones*, 375)

Later, of course, Jones is prompted to action after Northerton hits him over the head with a bottle, but his qualified romance plan to duel with Northerton is comically undercut by realistic details: the extravagant sum the sergeant demands for a sword, the sentinel's mistaking Jones for a ghost, and finally Northerton's escape.

From this point until Tom's decision to pursue Sophia after the Upton episode, the hero's journey is guided by random adventures characteristic of a picaresque novel: he and Partridge venture from inn to inn, are plagued by inclement weather, by hunger, and by poverty. Jones, nevertheless, retains something of the romance hero. Like Joseph, he is thought to be a gentleman at the inn where Northerton injured him, yet the inferences based on his appearance of gentility cease when Tom himself confesses he has no money to pay his bills. Later, Partridge spreads rumors that Tom is Allworthy's son, and these hints of Tom's gentility take hold because Partridge's greed and the greed of the innkeepers will it to be so. Even though on second reading we know that Tom is not Allworthy's son, his appearance of gentility seems fitting, for it momentarily satisfies the romance suspense about his identity that runs throughout the novel. In effect, the appearance of Tom's gentility is a disguise, not unlike that in the Heliodoran novel; it keeps our minds focused on the complications that we expect to be unraveled by the end of the novel. Partridge's role thus changes from the amiable companion of the *picaro* (like Strap in *Roderick Random*) to an unwitting guide and agent who provides the key to the hero's identity.[10]

If Jones pursues a path of both romance and antiromance heroes, Sophia pursues the path of the conventional romance heroine. While the hero is setting off on his journey, Sophia escapes from Squire Western's estate and heads toward London. Thus both lovers are on a journey, but the journey does not define itself as the kind we have seen in the Heliodoran novel until after the Upton episode, a manipulation of historical chronology that intensifies narrative suspense.

Sophia's journey begins in 7.7, when, after the departure of Jones, it becomes apparent that her marriage to Blifil will be pressed the following morning. On the surface, Sophia's scheme to go to London appears merely to be an escape from the tyranny of her father— a common enough convention in eighteenth-century literature. But the narrator's commentary in 7.7 suggests a romance pattern as well. Noting that the heroine's desire to leave is easier than her maid's ability to execute the plan, the narrator observes: "when a Lady hath once taken a Resolution to run to a Lover, or to run from him, all Obstacles are considered Trifles" (*Tom Jones*, 352). The sentence makes no conscious reference to Jones; in fact, Sophia's situation is clearly the alternate phrase. But the narrator's very mention of the first alternative suggests again that there is some hope, in the overall pattern of the novel, that the hero and heroine will be reunited: that Sophia will follow in the footsteps of a Heliodoran novel heroine. By the flash backward in book 10, after the Upton episode, it is clear that Sophia is consciously following the hero. When she learns where Jones's path has led him, she sets forth in pursuit. Later, when Jones in turn pursues Sophia, we realize that the hint of romance conventionality is not mere coincidence. Before we can make sense of the convention, however, we must sift through the antiromance appearance of the plot.

In the Heliodoran novel we expect the hero to be subjected to the lustful overtures of various ladies but to survive them with his fidelity intact. It is evidently a mark of the hero's virility to be thus tested and a mark of his integrity and love for the heroine to resist the temptations. Tom, of course, fails the romance test by making a "kind of Dutch Defense" against Mrs. Waters in the "Battle of the amorous Kind" at Upton. Yet, after he receives the muff Sophia sent to his unoccupied bed, he sets forth "in Quest of his lovely Sophia, whom he now resolved never to abandon the Pursuit of" and to whom "he now vowed eternal Constancy" (*Tom Jones, 554*).

With Tom's resolve established, Fielding turns the narrative back to Sophia. We learn the antecedent history of Sophia's journey to Upton; we hear Mrs. Fitzpatrick's history; and we witness Sophia being confused as a potential princess, Jenny Cameron.[11] Thus, when the narrative returns to Jones in 12.3, we find Tom in the throes of a love madness—determined, despite Partridge's urging to the contrary, to follow once again the footsteps of a romance hero:

> Since it is absolutely impossible for me to pursue any farther the Steps of my Angel—I will pursue those of Glory. Come on, my brave Lad, now for the Army:—It is a glorious Cause, and I would willingly sacrifice my Life in it, even tho' it was worth my preserving. (*Tom Jones*, 627)

Although "by mere Chance" Tom follows Sophia's path, his resolve is not unlike Justinian's in the *Ibrahim* or Artamène's in the *Cyrus,* both of whom seek heroic glory when love seems impossible. In a heroic novel Tom's resolve would be followed by a lengthy series of conquests that would inspire our admiration and confirm our expectations that the hero's seemingly impossible hopes will be granted. Instead of a heroic quest, however, Fielding presents two episodes that brand Tom's heroism as sentimental, not military: his discovery of Sophia's pocket book in 12.4 and his encounter with the highwayman in 12.14.

When Tom discovers the pocket book found by the beggar, it

turns his thoughts from military glory back to Sophia. The scene is sentimentally analogous to Cyrus's or Ibrahim's military heroism in that it serves as a rhetorical pause in the action that defines the quality of Tom's love: "He no sooner read the Name [of Sophia], than he prest it close to his Lips; nor could he avoid falling into some very frantic Raptures, notwithstanding his Company" (*Tom Jones*, 631). By not detailing the raptures, Fielding avoids overt sentimentalism, but the omission nevertheless stresses a rekindling of sentimental and romance hopes. In the succeeding paragraph Fielding makes Tom's response slightly ridiculous. He mumbles the pocket book "as if he had an excellent brown butter'd Crust in his Mouth, or as if he had really been a Bookworm, or an Author, who had nothing to eat but his own Works" (*Tom Jones*, 631-32). Later the book and the 100-pound banknote it contains become a reminder of Tom's quest. He refuses to deliver it to the highwayman in 12.14, even though he eventually offers the robber two or three guineas of his own meager funds. Later Tom twice refuses to cash in the banknote when he is in pecuniary difficulties—once on the road and once in London. It becomes, in short, a symbol of his romance hopes.

Tom's actions in this phase of the novel clearly do not measure up to the heroic actions of a conventional romance hero. He insists in 12.9, for example, on using the very side-saddle that Sophia used when she left Upton. Yet, when Tom meets the highwayman, his benevolent action suggests a sentimental heroism that supplants conventional heroism. Having bravely (and perhaps foolhardily) defended Sophia's banknote from the robber, Tom is moved to generosity as well as forgiveness by the affecting story of the highwayman's family. Although a chance circumstance here, Fielding consciously links the episode with the resolution of the plot. The highwayman turns out to be Mrs. Miller's cousin, and Tom's generosity toward him is one of the bits of evidence that prompt Mrs. Miller to defend Tom. In the chain of causal circumstances that develop in the novel, Fielding sets up a providential schema in which Jones, acting in accord with his good nature, redeems himself.[12]

Conclusion

The romance pattern that I have traced in *Tom Jones* sheds light on an important facet of the novel's meaning that has recently been approached from an entirely different angle. Wolfgang Iser, John Preston, and others argue that the delight and instruction of Fielding's novel emerge from the reader's participation in the process of discernment that Fielding invites the reader to undergo.[13] In effect, they argue that the meaning of the novel is not so much what Jones discovers about wisdom or about his birth as it is the training of our powers of judgment.

The romance elements, I contend, train us how to read the kind of history Fielding presents. As the narrator makes clear in the prefatory chapter to book 9, the history he is writing differs from romances not so much in a strict allegiance to records as in the genius, learning, and conversation with human nature that are requisite for a writer who presumes to invent good stories and tell them well. Fictional history for Fielding is thus predicated on the kind of rhetorical control that writers in the Heliodoran tradition sought by reshaping romance into a consciously unified plot that at once delights and instructs. Fielding maintains this control by giving his history a fundamentally romance pattern. Although we are witness to Tom's imprudence and to the causally similar consequences of those actions, the very suggestion of a romance potential in his character prompts us to expect a romance conclusion. Just as we become participants in the moral debate that runs through the novel, by having to entertain the opinions of both good- and ill-natured critics, so we must simultaneously entertain both a romance faith in the happy outcome of the novel and a historical faith in the *probability* of the outcome.

Our sentimental belief in Tom's goodness of heart thus becomes analogous to our belief in the idealized virtue of a romance hero. Even though Tom fails to be a paragon, his union with Sophia joins us, so to speak, with the wisdom implicit in the heroine's name. It is a wisdom based not on books—romance, historical, or philosophical—but on Fielding's third criterion for writers: conversance with human nature and all of its imperfections.

6

Romance and Irresolution in *Amelia*

In the *Covent-Garden Journal* of 28 January 1752, Fielding defends *Amelia* from attacks at the "Court of Censorial Inquiry" by commenting on its background:

> I have followed the Rules of all those who are acknowledged to have writ best on the Subject; and if her conduct be fairly examined, she will be found to deviate very little from the strictest Observation of those Rules; neither Homer nor Virgil pursued them with greater Care than myself, and the candid and learned Reader will see that the latter was the noble Model, which I made use of on this Occasion.[1]

By claiming Vergil as his "noble Model," Fielding seems to be turning away from the kind of comic history and comic romance he wrote in *Joseph Andrews* and *Tom Jones* and moving toward the serious epic. The numerous Vergilian echoes in the novel, such as the *in medias res* beginning, confirm this movement.[2] Yet despite these echoes, *Amelia* is guided as much by the conventions of romance and history as it is by the conventions of the classical epic. Indeed, Fielding blends epic, romance, and history together in this his last novel, with a seriousness that is unsettling to readers accustomed to the comic pose he assumes in his earlier novels.[3]

In *Joseph Andrews* the "rules" of the comic epic in prose are, by and large, a means of fusing romance and history. We are presented with causal-similar events sifted comically through a romance pattern that leads to a providentially ordered wish-fulfillment. In *Tom Jones* we witness a world in which romance assumptions and romance literary patterns qualify the misconceived empirical data surrounding the hero. The romance pattern redeems him from the causal-similar results of his imprudence and lands him at last on the "shore of Happiness"—the principal aim of a comic work.

In *Amelia* the fictional world is quite different and, as a result, the assumptions of both romance and history are used in strikingly different ways. As in *Joseph Andrews* and *Tom Jones,* the characters and situations at times suggest a romance that is set in a causally similar universe. Booth's story of his and Amelia's love, the objections of Mrs. Harris to their marriage, the intercession of Dr. Harrison, Booth's concealing himself in a wine hamper, and the lovers' eventual attempt to elope all belong to a tradition that can only be described as romanesque. The resolution, in which Amelia's birthright is restored, owes its allegiance to the same tradition, but the ending of *Amelia* does not satisfy our romance expectations the same way Fielding's other novels do.

Although the good characters in *Amelia* suffer from complications caused by villainous characters, the villainous ones are so pervasive and so connected with one another that they seem more a realistic picture of a corrupt and venal society than the archetypal agents of romance. The noble lord's attempt to seduce Amelia, for example, parallels his seduction of Mrs. Bennet earlier. He has carried on in the same way with Mrs. Trent and will presumably continue to do so until he is consumed with syphilis. He is, in fact, symptomatic of a disease that has taken over society. The noble lord's method of seducing Amelia parallels Colonel James's method. Indeed, like the lord, James leads Booth from one false promise to another, using his own wife as a bawd, just as the peer used Mrs. Ellison.

There is only a generalized triumph of justice at the end—no direct punishment of the villains for the harm they have done to the hero and heroine. No romance conclusion can restore order to this world. We are given some sense of poetic justice at the end: the good are rewarded, and the evil suffer the natural consequences of their particular corruptions. Yet there is a creeping suspicion that society remains corrupt. Although Booth, Amelia, their children, and Dr. Harrison find a happy-ever-after in the country, it is an escape, not a triumph, a private, not a public celebration.

Romance, Realism, and the Serious Epic in Prose

If *Amelia* is an epic, it is so not because Fielding imitates Vergil, but because, like the Heliodoran novelists, he follows the "Rules of all those who are acknowledged to have writ best on the Subject."

For the Heliodoran novelists, the prose epic combined the conscious design of the verse epic with the looseness of romance, allowing the writer to achieve, at once, unity and diversity, verisimilitude and the marvelous, instruction and delight.

Fielding demonstrates a similar concern for these matters in the very first chapter: "Containing the Exordium, etc." The first sentence, in fact, echoes the first line of the *Aeneid:* "The various Accidents which befel a very worthy Couple after their uniting in the State of Matrimony will be the Subject of the following History" (*Amelia,* 15). "Accidents" here parallels Vergil's metonymous *arma;* "a worthy Couple" replaces *virum;* and "History" parallels *cano.* After this first sentence, however, Fielding seems more concerned with the typical concerns of the prose epic than the verse epic. In sentence two, he comments on the instruction, delight, verisimilitude, and the marvelous to be found in his history:

> The Distresses which they waded through were some of them so exquisite, and the Incidents which produced these so extraordinary, that they seemed to require not only the utmost Malice, but the utmost Invention which Superstition ever attributed to Fortune: Tho' whether any such Being interfered in the case, or, indeed, whether there be any such Being in the Universe, is a Matter which I by no Means presume to determine in the Affirmative. (*Amelia,* 15)

That the distresses should be "exquisite" suggests a sentimental response that substitutes for the delight readers found in earlier romances. That they should be so extraordinary and so invented as to appear the malicious product of Fortune suggests the marvelous. Moreover, by his unwillingness to affirm whether Fortune exists, Fielding stresses the truth of his invention. We accuse Fortune, he tells us, for accidents that may have occurred by "natural Means"— "by quitting the Directions of Prudence, and following the blind Guidance of a predominant Passion" (*Amelia,* 16). To struggle against a tendency to accuse fortune for one's troubles is the instruction that comes from carefully examining life: "To retrieve the ill Consequences of a foolish Conduct, and by struggling manfully with Distress to subdue it, is one of the noblest efforts of wisdom and virtue" (*Amelia,* 16).

Thus Fielding asserts, although not in a formulaic way, that a history should delight and should contain instances of the marvelous, but that it should also make probable what is extraordinary, and instructive what is delightful. The final paragraph of the chapter, which I have already cited in chapter 1, synthesizes this dichotomy:

Life may as properly be called an Art as any other; and the great Incidents in it are no more to be considered as mere Accidents, than the several Members of a fine Statue, or a noble Poem. The Critics in all these are not content with knowing why and how it came to be so. By examining carefully the several Gradations which conduce to bring every Model to Perfection, we learn to know that Science in which the Model is formed: As Histories of this Kind, therefore, may properly be called Models of HUMAN LIFE, so by observing minutely the several Incidents which tend to the Catastrophe or Completion of the whole, and the minute Causes whence those Incidents are produced, we shall best be instructed in this most useful of all Arts, which I call the ART of LIFE. (*Amelia*, 17)

By urging us to examine the minute causes of incidents tending toward a catastrophe or a completion, Fielding urges us to see the design of history, just as we see the design of a fine poem, as a unity whose parts contribute to a whole. Such a statement is a manifesto about controlled realism, not unlike Scudéry's pronouncements in the preface to *Ibrahim:* "Every art hath its certain rules, which by infallible means lead to the ends proposed" (Scudéry, 1).

Because *Amelia* is a serious history, not a comic one, the way Fielding controls the fictional reality of the parts differs dramatically from his techniques in *Joseph Andrews* and *Tom Jones*. In those novels, unity and attendant conventions, such as suspense and agnorisis, were implicit in the kind of story being told, not explicit in the manner of telling it. Both novels are unified, but resolution arises from comic accident, and suspense from the narrator's ability to convince us of good nature's redeeming power. In *Amelia,* at least at first, the very manner of telling is an external contrivance, not unlike that in the Heliodoran novel: we are launched into the middle of things by virtue of Booth's imprisonment and his lengthy recital of antecedent action. We are also thrust into the middle of a marriage, a significant departure from *Joseph Andrews* and *Tom Jones,* as well as from the Heliodoran novel tradition. Instead of the adventures of a hero and heroine whom we expect to be married in the final chapter, we have a married couple, enduring not a physical journey with attendant separations and reunions, but a metaphorical one. The novel starts in the middle of what would be, if structured differently, a conventional happy-ever-after.

This unconventional change of narrative formula—the history of a marriage, not the history of lovers—necessarily means a different narrative attitude toward romance conventions. While Booth may be said to be enticed by a Dido-like Miss Matthews, while he may be said to be caught between the Scylla of his own predominant passion and the Charybdis of seeking a fortune, the novel, like the

Aethiopica, is an epic of both lovers. As a consequence, Fielding's approach to narrative structure is quite different from that of novels such as *Joseph Andrews* and *Tom Jones.* The chronological nature and hidden design of these novels made it necessary to sift character psychology through a reflective narrator. One does not attend so much to what Joseph, Fanny, Tom, and Sophia feel or think. By and large, we have been programmed to think and feel for them. In *Amelia,* however, we are witness to Booth's thoughts, without significant narrative intrusions until book 4, when the action returns to the present tense. Whatever tedium that narrative choice might produce, it forces us to see the history through Booth's sensibility. From book 4 on, the narrator presents conflicts as internal—the consequences of Booth's affair with Miss Matthews and of his financial imprudence.

Restructuring the comic-romance pattern of *Joseph Andrews* and *Tom Jones* places a greater emphasis on sentimentalism. In Fielding's earlier novels, sentimentalism is almost always comically deflected. Our belief in Tom Jones's goodness of heart, for example, virtually dictates a sentimental reunion at the end of the novel. Yet Fielding manages to keep our sentimental response comic by making him enough of a romance hero to inspire our hopes for his happiness. Thus our expectations are as much programmed by poetic justice as by sentimental justice. In *Amelia,* Fielding's very purpose is sentimental. Whereas in *Tom Jones* he finds a way to reconcile history to a romance pattern, in *Amelia* Fielding's realistic depiction of vice and corruption suggests irresolution, not completion. The novel fails, by and large, to make that irresolution thematically successful (as later, more realistic novels do) because the bitter realities of the world outlast the romance ending.

Booth's Recital and the Heliodoran Structure

Unlike the design of Fielding's comic histories, where the unity is more evident upon reseeing than on first sight, *Amelia's in medias res* beginning makes us aware, from the start, of a consciously contrived structure. Like the Heliodoran novel, such a beginning establishes a dramatic framework. We wonder what accidents brought the hero and heroine to so calamitous a circumstance, and we are held in suspense as to how the novel will end. To use Amyot's term, the epic-style opener creates a "liaison" between beginning and middle and between middle and end.

In one sense Booth's imprisonment, his recital of the antecedent history, and his infidelity with Miss Matthews establish the same kind of liaison. When Booth's recital ends in book 4, we are held in suspense both because Booth is unwilling to confess his transgression to Amelia and because Matthews continues to lust for him. His failure to confess his infidelity produces immediate suspense; Matthews's continuing lust is a long-range source of complications, leading to Booth's arrest in book 12 and also to the hero's and heroine's final reconciliation. In a larger sense, the story Booth tells in his recital sets up a liaison between his romance love for Amelia and the realistic present, in which he is unfaithful.

Curiously, Booth's recital compresses the four stages of the Heliodoran novel. It establishes a romance perspective that is made all the more unrealistic as the characters face difficulties that arise from deeply rooted corruptions in society.

As in the Heliodoran novel, Booth's love for Amelia develops because he perceives her as exalted among all the women of the world. Her excellent qualities, however, are qualified—not in the comic manner of Fanny in *Joseph Andrews,* but in a sentimental manner. Like a conventional romance hero, Booth admired Amelia from afar without, initially, any spark of love. Indeed, because she was courted by men of the "highest Rank" and "great Fortune," she seems absolutely out of his reach (*Amelia,* 66). Her beauty is qualified when, after a chaise accident, her nose is "beat all to pieces," causing her to appear less than attractive to fashionable society.[4] This accident, however minute, prompts Booth to act as a sentimental champion. When one of the ladies of the town sarcastically abuses Amelia for her broken nose, Booth defends her as the most beautiful woman in England—a reply that the ladies regard as rude and that wins Booth Amelia's affection.

Like Theagenes and Periandro, Booth is initially reticent in his love—not for lack of passion, but because he feels that his "poor Provision of an Ensign's Commission" makes him unworthy of loving Amelia. This feeling of unworthiness leads him to resolve "never to propose Love to her seriously" (*Amelia,* 68). This resolution, combined with the conventional objection of Amelia's mother, produces something akin to the love malady that afflicts characters in the Heliodoran novel. After Mrs. Harris discovers Booth's love for her daughter and denies him entry to her house, he tries to "cure" himself of his malady.

In the Heliodoran tradition, the love malady convention was designed to turn "scorners" of love into lovers; that is, it alerts the lover to an intensity of feeling that is beyond reason's power to control. In *Amelia* Fielding associates Booth's unsuccessful attempt to cure himself with Booth's belief in the doctrine of predominant passions. He tells Miss Matthews:

> those know little of real Love or Grief, who do not know how much we deceive ourselves when we pretend to aim at the Cure of either. It is with these, as it is with some Distempers of the Body, nothing is, in the least, agreeable to us but what serves to heighten the Disease (*Amelia*, 76)

By giving himself over to an exquisiteness of feeling, Booth becomes a hero whose sentimental nature—whose feelings—supplant the heroic resolve of an Ibrahim or a Cyrus.

Indeed, as Booth attempts to visit Amelia despite Mrs. Harris's objections, there are further suggestions of conventional romance behavior. None of these, however, sufficiently resolve the realistic dilemma the lovers face. After Booth and Amelia are separated because of Mrs. Harris, for example, Amelia is "kept a close Prisoner," not unlike Chariclea in the court of Caricles. Indeed, not unlike Calasiris in Heliodorus's novel, who inquires into Theagenes' background when he discovers the heroine's love, Dr. Harrison examines Booth's intentions about Amelia in order to make sure that the hero is not bent on "stealing a human Creature for the sake of her fortune" (*Amelia*, 78). When he is assured of Booth's love, Harrison becomes their "Friend and zealous Advocate." After Mrs. Harris decides to marry Amelia to Mr. Winckworth, a "great Squire" with a coach and six, Dr. Harrison formulates the daring but ineffectual romance plan of Booth's concealing himself in a wine hamper.[5]

Harrison's intercession, although not the plan itself, parallels Calasiris's plan that Theagenes elope with Chariclea after her adoptive father had made plans to marry her off to another suitor. Later, in the present action of the novel, Harrison continues to serve a romance function similar to that of Calasiris, and even to that of Parson Adams. Even though Dr. Harrison loses faith in Booth, he is still a father figure for both hero and heroine, aiding them in numerous financial difficulties.

There are further suggestions of romance convention in Booth's account of his and Amelia's love. When the hero and heroine elope, they see themselves not only in Spanish romance roles, as Baker points out,[6] but they also disguise themselves in rags provided by Mrs. Atkinson. Although there is a causal reason for their assuming different clothes (they were caught in a rainstorm), Booth himself characterizes Amelia's appearance in terms that recall the disguises assumed by Heliodoran novel heroines: "Amelia, in the poor Rags of her old Nurse, looked scarce less beautiful than I have seen her appear at a Ball or an Assembly" (*Amelia*, 85). Like the Heliodoran heroine, Amelia's natural beauty outshines even an ignoble appearance—at least in Booth's eyes.[7] The couple spend a chaste night, despite Mrs. Atkinson's supposition that they are married, and they speak in French, another disguise, in order to make their plans.

A quick sketch of Booth's history from their marriage until their move to London demonstrates both a resemblance to the Heliodoran novel pattern and a departure from it. The hero and heroine are separated because Booth, like Cyrus and Ibrahim, is a soldier. The separation itself leads to conventional tears, agonies, and despair on Amelia's part. Like a conventional hero, Booth is torn between love and honor, yet Fielding manipulates matters so that Booth, unlike the typical romance hero, has a real choice between the two. Shortly before his regiment received orders to go to Gibraltar, Booth had arranged to exchange his commission with an officer from a regiment that was unlikely to be ordered abroad. By the time Booth's regiment receives its orders, the transfer had not yet been officially signed. Even though the other officer is willing to complete the exchange, Booth is torn between his love for Amelia and his honor as a soldier:

> I was now reduced to a Dilemma, the most dreadful which I think any Man can experience; in which I am not ashamed to own, I found Love was not so overmatched by Honour as he ought to have been. The thoughts of leaving Amelia in her present Condition, to Misery, perhaps to Death or Madness, were insupportable; nor could any other Consideration but that, which now tormented me on the other Side, have combated them a moment. (*Amelia*, 93)

By rendering the love-honor conflict in this way, Fielding translates the conventional romance conflict into a sentimental one. Not only does Amelia represent sentimental love (in 5.2 she paints a picture of Booth's and her happiness in the smallest of huts, a paradise far from the world of honor), but Booth himself is sensible of his sentimental duties.

The separation of the lovers ends when Amelia follows Booth to Gibraltar, a decision that demonstrates a willfulness akin to Chariclea's in the *Aethiopica* and Isabelle's in the *Ibrahim*.[8] Once reunited, the lovers embark on a journey of sorts back to England and are afflicted with calamities that initially parallel the Heliodoran pattern. A rival, M. Bagillard, pursues Amelia and provides a brief period of narrative conflict. Even the conventional obstacle of parental objection affects them on the journey. Betty Harris, allegedly acting on the wishes of her and Amelia's deceased mother, cuts the lovers off from all financial assistance.

With financial troubles besetting the hero and heroine, the conventional pattern of the narrative begins to change. Initially, the question of money seems an external narrative conflict, not unlike the tempests and shipwrecks in the Heliodoran novel. In fact, like Periandro and Auristela when faced with tempests or shipwrecks, Booth and Amelia seek a haven: the farm provided for them by Dr. Harrison. Booth describes this haven as an "earthly Paradise" (*Amelia*, 145), noting that their lives at that point "resembled a calm sea" (*Amelia*, 147). But because of Booth's own imprudence in managing the farm, they leave this haven and head for another one, surrounded by more tempestuous seas—the verge of the court.

The romance elements in Booth's recital, of course, do not control the plot, as analogous conventions in *Tom Jones* and *Joseph Andrews* do. They serve, rather, to highlight a romance potential in the novel that is consistently thwarted by more realistic factors. After Amelia and Booth escape from Mrs. Harris, for example, the journey of betrothed lovers that seems imminent is thwarted by Mrs. Harris's consent to the marriage. Suggestions of romance conventions survive in the rest of Booth's narration, but the details become increasingly more realistic as we get closer to the present action of the novel.

Characters and the Heliodoran Tradition

By the time Booth's recital ends, we have witnessed the beginning of a romance pattern whose conventional ending (a marriage) is really the midpoint of the action. In the balance of the novel we shall see enough parallels with the Heliodoran novel to expect a romance conclusion, but we shall also see several differences in Fielding's management of plot and characterization. Although both characters suffer through conventional romance complications, our romance interests focus more on Amelia than on Booth. From book 4 onward, Fielding emphasizes the realistic consequences of Booth's infidelity and of his consistent lack of good judgment. The action concerning him is thus guided by causality. The action concerning Amelia, however, is guided by the narrative analogy to divine providence. As a result, the character of Amelia prompts us to expect a romance conclusion, even though the character of Booth prompts us to expect a series of realistic consequences.

In a conventional romance, the hero is brave, faithful, and chaste. Our romance expectations for his happiness, in fact, partly result from his ability to demonstrate these qualities. Even in *Tom Jones,* in which the hero, like Booth, is unfaithful, our disapproval of Tom's

actions is counterbalanced by our belief in his goodness and by a
pervading expectation that he and Sophia will eventually find
happiness. In *Amelia,* however, we are ever conscious not only of
Booth's failure, but also of his more realistic sense of guilt. Later
in the novel his seductress, Miss Matthews, will become a source
of fairly conventional complications for the hero and heroine. Yet
when Booth actually commits adultery, Fielding's attention is on the
sentimental reality of Booth's action.

Unlike the narrator in *Tom Jones,* who deflects our attention
away from Tom's affairs with Molly Seagrim and Mrs. Waters by
making the hero a comic victim, the narrator in *Amelia* attributes
Booth's lapse to realistic causes:

> We desire . . . the good-natured and candid Reader will be pleased
> to weigh attentively the several unlucky Circumstances which
> concurred so critically, that Fortune seemed to have used her utmost
> Endeavours to ensnare Booth's Constancy. Let the Reader set before
> his Eyes a fine young Woman, in a manner, a first Love, conferring
> Obligations and using every Art to soften, to allure, to win, and to
> enflame; let him consider the Time and Place; let him remember that
> Mr. Booth was a young Fellow, in the highest Vigour of Life; and,
> lastly, let him add one single Circumstance, that the Parties were
> alone together, and then, if he will not acquit the Defendant, he must
> be convicted; for I have nothing more to say in his Defense. (*Amelia,*
> 154)

Fielding's emphasis on fortune early in the paragraph seemingly
contradicts his admonition against blaming fortune for events that
have natural causes. But the explanations at the end—Booth's youthful
vigor; Matthews's ability to soften, allure, win, and inflame; and,
more important, the circumstances of time and place—all force us
to see the event as the inevitable result of Booth's limited heroism
acting in a causally similar world.

When the narrator further analyzes Booth's week of "criminal
Conversation" with Matthews, he emphasizes the very weakness of
Booth's heroism:

> Repentance never failed to follow his Transgressions; and yet so perverse
> is our Judgment, and so slippery is the Descent of Vice, when once
> we are entered into it; the very same Crime which he now repented
> of became a Reason for doing that which was to cause his future
> Repentance; and he continued to sin on because he had begun. (*Amelia,*
> 155)

Tom's bedding Mrs. Waters in 9.5 of *Tom Jones* is made humorous
by the "Battle of the amorous Kind" that preceded it. The narrator
makes us think of the mock-heroic nature of Tom's surrender: "To

confess the Truth, I am afraid Mr. Jones maintained a Kind of Dutch Defence, and treacherously delivered up the Garrison without duly weighing his allegiance to the fair Sophia" (*Tom Jones*, 513). In the prefatory essay that intervenes between Tom's surrender and Sophia's arrival at Upton, Fielding mitigates Tom's guilt. We are warned "not to condemn a Character as a bad one, because he is not a perfectly good one" (*Tom Jones*, 526). In *Amelia,* however, Fielding stresses the psychological effects of Booth's culpable nature:

> In fact, if we regard this World only, it is in the interest of every Man to be either perfectly good, or completely bad. He had better destroy his Conscience than gently wound it. The many bitter Reflections which every bad Action costs a Mind in which there are any Remains of Goodness are not to be compensated by the highest Pleasures which such an Action can produce. (*Amelia*, 155)

Fielding's emphasis here is on the sentimental psychology of guilt. We are asked to think about the effects that Booth's conscience implicitly has on his sensibility. Even though he repents and "continues to sin on, because he had begun," nevertheless his repentance, the narrator tells us, "returned still heavier and heavier, till at last it flung him into a melancholy" (*Amelia*, 155). The "Melancholy" is thus a displacement of the conventional hero's self-confidence in his constancy. Booth is unable to confess his sin to Amelia, and in not doing so, he leaves himself open to Matthews's later machinations. She thus becomes a rival to Amelia and the source of later complications. Notably, she does not possess any extraordinary powers like her Heliodoran counterparts. Her only power rests in her being a threat to Booth's sentimental affection for Amelia, a reminder to him of his own unworthiness. Indeed, Booth's inability to remove Matthews completely from his thoughts becomes the principal source of suspense in the novel.

Curiously, Fielding later gives the suspense created by Booth's guilt a romance quality. He is the object of false rumors—not unlike those in the *Cyrus* or *Tom Jones.* At the end of the novel, just before Trent has Booth arrested, the hero is once again revisited by the specter of Miss Matthews, whom he consents to visit so that he may, at last, be rid of her. While he is visiting her, Colonel James sends a letter that Amelia reads, challenging Booth to a duel. James is trying to seduce Amelia, and at the same time he is angry with Booth for visiting Miss Matthews (who rejected James). The letter, although addressed to Booth, was intended for Amelia's eyes, and it creates the same kind of confusion as do the rumored infidelities in the Heliodoran novel. Booth, though guilty of infidelity earlier, is unjustly accused by a rival at a point in the novel when even Amelia—all patient and all-forgiving Amelia—momentarily doubts him. After she receives the letter from James and a subsequent one from the imprisoned Booth, Amelia suffers the kind of despair we expect of a conventional heroine:

> she passed a miserable and sleepless Night, her gentle Mind torn and distracted with various and contending Passions, distressed with Doubts, and wandering in a kind of Twilight, which presented her only Objects of different Degrees of Horrour, and where black Despair closed at a small Distance the gloomy prospect. (*Amelia*, 493)

The gloomy prospect, which is closed by black despair, forebodes the end of romance. In the light of day, however, Amelia brings herself out of despair by flattering herself that Booth was "less guilty than she imagined," a quality of her ameliorative temperament that allows this complication to be resolved.

After Booth finally confesses his earlier infidelity and explains his innocence on this occasion, Amelia tells him that she has long since known about his infidelity (Miss Matthews has sent her a letter, trying, like Lady Bellaston in *Tom Jones,* to avenge herself by exposing the hero's transgression). The rumor that Booth had been unfaithful a second time is thus resolved by Amelia's almost too-understanding forgiveness. She tells Booth that she made "large Allowances" for the circumstances of his infidelity and had forgotten Matthews's letter until Colonel James's awakened her doubts. Whereas in the Heliodoran novel supposed infidelity provides complications that are resolved in a poetically just manner, in *Amelia* the reconciliation takes place because of the heroine's forgiving good-nature. It is, as it were, sentimentally just.

In the Heliodoran novel, rival lovers serve two conventional purposes: they provide narrative conflict that impedes the journey, and they provide internal conflicts for the hero and heroine that illustrate their love and fidelity to one another. Moreover, the actions of rivals are virtually formulaic. Typically, a nobleman falls in love with the heroine; she resists by virtue of her wit and her chastity, but the very presence of the rival produces a temporary fit of jealousy in the hero. When the threat of the rival is removed, the hero and heroine are stronger in their vows. Given the stylized rhetoric of romance, the rivals pose verisimilar threats: they embody real human passions such as lust, power, and fraud. Their authentic villainy, however, is no match for the inevitable fidelity of the hero and heroine. A seductress may pursue the hero, but we expect him to resist her because he is a hero. A nobleman may attack the heroine, may even abduct her, but we expect that her chastity will be preserved intact. Even when Fielding inverts the convention in *Tom Jones,* our romance expectations are still controlled by romance expectations—by Tom's higher love for Sophia.

As we have seen, Miss Matthews's seduction of Booth defines his limitations as a hero. The rivals pursuing Amelia, however, are far more conventional. They define her as a paragon of sentimental virtue. The unnamed peer and Colonel James produce more melodramatic complications, which cause the heroine to respond in a conventional way.

The unnamed peer, for instance, prompts Booth to conventional jealousy and Amelia to an assertion of virtue's conventional power:

> O Mr. Booth! Mr. Booth! you must well know that a Woman's Virtue is always her sufficient Guard. No Husband, without suspecting that can suspect any Danger from those Snares you mention—And why, if you are liable to take such things into your Head, may not your Suspicions fall on me, as well as on any other? for sure nothing was ever more unjust, I will not say ungrateful, than the Suspicions which you have bestowed on his Lordship. (*Amelia*, 251)

Amelia's belief that virtue is a sufficient guard signals that romance convention is at work, at least on her part. She fails, initially, to recognize the peer's villainy, however, because he does not play by romance rules. He disguises his seduction by pretending an affection for Amelia's children—an assault at the very core of Amelia's sentimental nature. And were it not for Mrs. Bennet's history, Amelia might easily become another victim of the peer, despite the guard of her virtue.[9] Fielding's method seems clear. He moves us away from the semblance of romance convention (Amelia's assurance of virtue's power) to a recognition that romance beliefs do not apply in the corrupt society represented by the lord. Virtue itself is an insufficient guard. To combat a villain such as the lord, the heroine must have a knowledge of his utter depravity and an ability to deceive him—as she does later, with Mrs. Bennet's help.

Amelia's more developed understanding of human vice allows her to see through the other rival, Colonel James. Pretending an affection for Booth, James tries to get Booth to accept a commission in the West Indies, so that James himself will have Amelia in his power. Although Booth regards James as an ally, James is as potentially treacherous as the noble lord. Curiously, Amelia puts on the appearance of cordiality to James, even though she knows his designs, lest Booth be prompted to act heroically and duel with his rival:

to avoid giving any Umbrage to her Husband, Amelia was forced
to act in a Manner which she was conscious must give Encouragement
to the Colonel: a Situation which perhaps requires as great Prudence
and Delicacy as any in which the heroic Part of the female Character
can be exerted. (*Amelia*, 363)

Amelia is thus ironically cast in a role analogous to Heliodoran novel
heroines, who pretend a willingness to accept a rival's overtures in
order to preserve their own and the hero's safety.[10]

The rivals in *Amelia* not only produce conventional conflicts,
but they are also themselves symptoms of a corruption in society
that can only be escaped, not conquered. Both in terms of the narrative
complications and in terms of the corruption they represent in society,
their villainy leads to the final distresses of the novel. After Mrs.
Bennet-Atkinson rescues Amelia from the noble lord's talons by taking
Amelia's place at the masquerade, the lord instructs Trent, as his
pimp, to enforce a debt Booth had been tricked into. To secure money
for this debt, Amelia pawns all her belongings, but Booth, in his
usual imprudent manner, gives the money to a "great man" in vain
hopes, once again, of buying a commission. This action paves the
way for Trent to have Booth arrested. Simultaneously, Miss Matthews
reappears and threatens to write to Amelia unless Booth comes to
see her. When Booth goes, he is followed by a spy of Colonel James,
whose jealousy about Matthews's affection for Booth causes James,
as I have mentioned, to write the treacherous letter that Amelia
reads while Booth is imprisoned.

Thus, when Booth is arrested, there is a concatenation of
circumstances—all plausible and all resulting either from Booth's
imprudence or the treachery of others—that makes a catastrophe
imminent. Indeed, as in the penultimate stage of the Heliodoran novel,
the hero seems in an inextricable dilemma. He is unable to pay his
debts, and his guilt about the Matthews affair plunges him into the
depths of despair. Even his long-patient advocate, Dr. Harrison, seems
unwilling to bail him out. As in the Heliodoran novel, the ending
we are given, however, is not a catastrophe, but a completion—
or at least a qualified completion. It involves a return to the kind
of romance incidents that occurred in Booth's opening recital.

Simultaneously with Booth's decision to visit Miss Matthews,
Amelia goes to a pawnbroker to sell her last possession: a portrait,
encrusted with gold and diamonds, that was supposed to be part of
the casket of trinkets that Amelia sent with Booth upon his departure
for Gibraltar. When Booth did not find the portrait, he and Amelia
speculated that Amelia's sister had stolen it. In fact, it was stolen

by Atkinson, the son of Amelia's nurse, a faithful companion to the hero and a sentimental lover-from afar of the heroine.

The reemergence of the portrait serves both a sentimental and a romance function. Amelia pawns it so that she can prepare a good, simple dinner for her husband (which he misses because he is at Matthews's). Pawning the portrait heightens suspense by dramatizing Amelia's sentimental willingness to sacrifice all for Booth's happiness at home and hearth. The portrait quickly becomes a key for unraveling the plot in the final book, however. Mr. Robinson by chance sees the portrait in the pawnshop, and by chance happens to be locked up by the same bailiff as Booth. Robinson is thus able to reveal how Amelia's sister, Miss Harris, had a lawyer forge their mother's will, depriving Amelia of her rightful legacy. Like Chariclea's silken ribbon, the portrait becomes tangible proof of the heroine's birthright, and it paves the way for the romance resolution of the plot: the payment of Booth's debts and the couple's return to a comfortable married life away from London.

The full completion, however, depends upon a reversal of Booth's identity as well. If Booth is still blind to prudence, Amelia's legacy will only produce further distresses. Fielding produces this part of the resolution in a somewhat heavy-handed way. Having professed a deistical belief in the doctrine of the passions, Booth is brought, at the brink of despair, to read Dr. Barrow's sermons, and these correct his former doubts about Christianity.

If there are vestiges of the picaresque in Booth's behavior, his conversion is conventional to that genre, yet it need not be looked at as such. In the *Aethiopica* and the *Persiles,* one of the thematic concerns running concurrent with the hero's and heroine's journey is a rectification of acceptable religious belief. Theagenes and Chariclea become priest and priestess of a new ritual in Meroe; Periandro and Auristela are returned to the true church of Rome. In a similar way, Booth's conversion from the doctrine of the passions to Dr. Harrison's and Amelia's Christianity provides a thematic resolution that parallels the narrative resolution. Restored to sentimental Christianity, Booth, in effect, is restored to Fielding's brand of good-natured Christian benevolence.

Conclusion

Despite the romance resolution, *Amelia* does not tend toward the kind of completion we might expect in a conventional romance. The happy-ever-after, the prediction of flourishing generations, and the restoration of Amelia's birthright all occur, but the ending brings us to a state of happiness that is arbitrary and sentimental. It is not so much that romance dreams are fulfilled, as that the nightmares of the real world have ceased.

Since reality is more sharply depicted in *Amelia* than in Fielding's other novels (perhaps, as some critics suggest, because of the author's gloom about his own failing powers),[11] the very conventions that make *Tom Jones* and *Joseph Andrews* gloriously satisfying make Fielding's last novel dissatisfying. The romance pattern that I have defined as Heliodoran is successful in Fielding's comic novels because it provides a conventional framework within which Fielding's pose as a historian can have free range.

In *Joseph Andrews* and *Tom Jones,* despite each work's avowed fidelity to empirical truth, we are aware that the endings signal romance assumptions and that therefore the unity of the novels must imply some romance structure. Joseph's marriage to Fanny results from a romance resolution to the problems of their identities; Tom's marriage to Sophia results from a revelation of his parentage and a final sorting out of his romance and antiromance behavior. By understanding the implicit romance structure of both novels, we can see how Fielding reshapes romance conventions so that they fit the causal pattern of history. The literary structure of romance thus converges with Fielding's notion of comedy: to land the principal characters "at last on the shore of happiness" (*Tom Jones*, 875). It is as if Fielding invigorates the literary conventions that became clichés in the heroic novel and uses them to create a new synthesis—a new type of epic in prose.

In *Amelia,* where Fielding consciously subjects the classical epic to historical causality, the conventional formula almost becomes a constraint. Perhaps the reason this novel fails is Fielding's inability to subordinate the conventional romance pattern to his description of the actual world of corruption. We sense that Amelia and Booth should be rewarded, but their romance happiness at the end is either too far distant narratively from the venality of London, or not far enough distant thematically. Fielding does not grapple with the artistic potential of irresolution, even though that is where he seems to be heading.

In the next century novelists such as Dickens will be able to subordinate romance patterns to the main theme and use them to to contrast more realistic elements. The romance love of Florence and Walter Gay in *Dombey and Son,* for instance, serves as a foil for the decaying world of the Dombey empire. Their marriage implies a narrative escape from Dombey, but thematically their escape is subordinate to the fall of the house of Dombey. Even more tellingly, we are aware at the end of *Hard Times* that Sissy Jupe will receive the conventional reward of marriage and children, but also that her happiness is subordinate to the pervasive unhappiness of Louisa and distinctly contrasts with it. In both of these cases, Dickens uses romance conventions to provide ameliorative relief without implying, as Fielding does in *Amelia,* that romance convention has resolved the problem. Fielding cannot dispose of the romance conventions because he must land Booth and Amelia on the shore of happiness, but he cannot at the same time make them consistent with what is most realistic about the novel.

Notes

Preface

1. Ian Watt, *The Rise of the Novel* (Berkeley: University of California Press, 1964), 13.

2. Ibid.

Chapter 1. Romance, Epic, and Fielding

1. There is no ready label for the sixteenth- and seventeenth-century works influenced by Heliodorus's *Aethiopica.* The closest term to *Heliodoran novel* existing is *novela bizantina*—a term Spanish literary historians use to refer to works, such as the *Persiles,* that imitate such postclassical Greek novels as the *Aethiopica,* Achilles Tatius's *Clitophon and Leucippe,* and Longus's *Daphnis and Chloe. Byzantine novel* is an unsatisfactory description, however, because Heliodorus's work antedates the civilization we usually think of as Byzantine. Moreover, while Achilles Tatius and Longus certainly influenced many sixteenth- and seventeenth-century works, the *Aethiopica* alone is the most frequently cited model for the epic in prose. For a discussion of the influence of Heliodorus on the Spanish *novela bizantina,* see Albinio Martín Gabriel, "Heliodoro y la novela española," *Cuadernos de Literatura* 8 (1950): 215-34. For recent studies of Heliodorus, see Arthur Heiserman, *The Novel Before the Novel* (Chicago: Chicago University Press, 1977); Gerald N. Sandy, *Heliodorus* (Boston: Twayne, 1982).

Although no extensive study of the influence of the *Aethiopica* on the history of the English novel has been done, references to it are plentiful. In her *Progress of Romance* (1798; reprint, New York: Garland, 1970), Clara Reeve discusses the *Aethiopica* as one of the "most ancient and famous Romances." It is important for historians to consider it, she notes, both because it is "indisputably a work of Genius" and because it derives from Homer (31-32). Contemporary historians of prose fiction have also noted its importance. See F. M. Warren, *A History of the Novel Previous to the Seventeenth Century* (New York: Henry Holt, 1895), 60-89; Ernest A. Baker, *The History of the English Novel* (1924; reprint, New York: Barnes and Noble, 1950), 1:22-23; Diana Neill, *A Short History of the English Novel* (1951; reprint, New York: Collier, 1964), 10-18; Charles C. Mish, ed., *Short Fiction of the Seventeenth Century* (New York: New York University Press, 1963), ix. Even in theoretical discussions such as Robert Scholes's and Robert Kellogg's *The Nature of Narrative* (New York: Oxford University Press, 1966), the influence of the *Aethiopica* and other Greek romances is recognized. See especially p. 68, where the authors note that the plot of *Tom Jones* is essentially a Greek-romance plot.

2. From the *Aethiopica*'s first translation into the vernacular by Jacques Amyot in 1547, it became associated with the classical epic and, indeed, became the model for the prose epic in the minds of many critics. Alban K. Forcione summarizes the critical responses of Amyot, Tasso, Scaliger, and El Pinciano in *Cervantes, Aristotle, and the Persiles* (Princeton: Princeton University Press, 1970), 55-87.

3. In the "Apologie for Poesie," Sir Philip Sidney cites the hero of the *Aethiopica* to exemplify his discussion of how poetry can deliver a "golden" world where nature exhibits a "brazen" one. Poetry, employing its "uttermost cunning," is capable of producing "so true a lover as *Theagines,* so constant a friend as *Pilades,* so excellent a lover as *Virgils Aeneas.*" See *Elizabethan Critical Essays,* ed. G. Gregory Smith (London: Oxford University Press, 1904), 1:157. Sidney also cites Heliodorus as an example of an "excellent poet" who never versified (159-60). For a discussion of the influence of Heliodorus on Sidney's *Arcadia,* see Samuel Lee Wolff, *The Greek Romances in Elizabethan Prose Fiction* (New York: Columbia University Press, 1912), 353-66; Margaret Schlauch, *Antecedents of the English Novel: 1400-1600* (London: Oxford University Press, 1965), 174-85; Walter R. Davis, *Idea and Act in Elizabethan Prose Fiction* (Princeton: Princeton University Press, 1969), 80-81, 157, 166-67.

4. Forcione traces Cervantes' criticism of romances in the *Quixote* to earlier critics in the Aristotelian revival who applied the standards of unity and verisimilitude in the classical epic to chivalric romance (11-45). What emerges in the writings of Pigna, Miturno, and Tasso is a movement toward legitimizing incidents of the marvelous. The Canon of Toledo, he argues further, accepts the Renaissance criticism of romances by condemning the chivalric romances for their lack of unity and verisimilitude, but the Canon also offers a new model that suggests a "purification" of romance of chivalry "in accordance with the dictates of Aristotelian-Horatian aesthetic criteria for the ideal epic" (100). For other discussions of sixteenth-century epic theory, see E. C. Riley, *Cervantes' Theory of the Novel* (Oxford: Clarendon Press, 1962), 50-56; E. M. W. Tillyard, *The English Epic and Its Background* (1954; reprint, New York: Oxford University Press, 1966), 222-33.

5. In the prologue to his *Novelas Ejemplares,* Cervantes links his final novel, *Persiles y Sigismunda* with the Aethiopica, describing it as a "libro que se atreve a competir con Heliodoro, si ya por atrevido no sale con las manos en la cabeza" ["a book that dares to compete with Heliodorus, if it doesn't, by its daring, disgrace itself" (translation mine)], vol. 1 of *Biblioteca de Autores Españoles* (Madrid, 1944), 100.

Various scholars have noted the extent of the Heliodoran influence on the *Persiles.* Rudolph Schevill, in "Studies in Cervantes: *Persiles y Sigismunda,*" *Modern Philology* 4 (1906), notes that the *Aethiopica* filled the gap during the period when "older forms of fiction were beginning to lose their hold and no new forms had sufficiently matured to take their place" (684). He cites correspondences between the *Aethiopica* and the *Persiles,* concentrating most particularly on the authors' techniques of keeping their characters in a mystery gradually to be cleared up as the novels progress (692). For further discussions of the influence of the *Aethiopica* on the *Persiles,* see William Atkinson, "The Enigma of the *Persiles,*" *Bulletin of Hispanic Studies* 24 (1947): 242-53; E. C. Riley, 130; Juan Bautista Avalle-Arce's introduction to the modern edition of the *Persiles* (Madrid: Clásicos Castalia, 1969), 22-23; Stansilav Zimic, "El *Persiles* como crítica de la novela bizantina," *Acta Neophilologica* 3 (1970): 49-64; Alban K. Forcione, *Cervantes' Christian Romance* (Princeton: Princeton University Press, 1972), 19.

6. In the preface to a seventeenth-century English translation of the *Aethiopica* by "A Person of Quality" and Nahum Tate (London, 1686), the translators observe the following about Heliodorus's influence:

> Besides the Testimonies of the Learned for my Author, it is yet to be added, That he was not only the first who attempted this way of Writing, but the Best. The *Cassandra* and *Cleopatra* of the French were Scions from this Stock, nor shall we envy them the Reputation which those Authors seemed chiefly to design, the diversion of the Ladies. Heliodorus has as well contrived for their favour, yet so as to make the Amour subordinate to the Instruction, and every where an occasion of dispensing that Learning and Experience, with which he was so furnished. The Philosophy and Politicks delivered in the Romance of *Barclay* have rendered it worthy of perusal of the greatest Statesman; yet, on the first view, we shall find the *Argenis* but a copy of *Chariclea*.

For a discussion of the *Argenis,* see Gerald Langford, "John Barclay's *Argenis:* a Seminal Novel," *Studies in English* 26 (1947): 59-76.

7. Charles Sorel, *The Extravagant Shepherd,* translated from the French (London, 1654), 13:52-58.

8. See A. F. B. Clark, *Jean Racine* (1939; reprint, New York: Octogon Books, 1969), 39.

9. For a discussion of Baltasar Gracián's *El Criticón,* see Theodore L. Kassier, *The Truth Disguised: Allegorical Structure and Technique in Gracián's El* Criticón (London: Tamesis, 1976), 20-29.

10. Arthur L. Cooke, in "Henry Fielding and the Writers of Heroic Romance," *PMLA* 62 (1947): 984-94, examines the possibility of Fielding's indebtedness to the theories of the prose epic that influenced writers such as La Calprenède and Scudéry. He concludes that Fielding either borrowed his theory about the comic epic from the heroic novelists and did not acknowledge his indebtedness, or that he derived his theory from a common source: the classical epic. Some critics, such as J. Paul Hunter, see parallels between Fielding's novels and the Homeric and Vergilian traditions of the epic; see *Occasional Form: Henry Fielding and the Chains of Circumstance* (Baltimore: Johns Hopkins University Press, 1975), 130-40. Yet studies of this sort focus primarily on the thematic or structural parallels that create, as it were, a new tradition of the epic rather than on a specific and continuing literary theory of the epic poem in prose. See also E. M. W. Tillyard, *The Epic Strain in the English Novel* (London: Chatto and Windus, 1963), 51-58; Thomas E. Maresca, *Epic to Novel* (Columbus: Ohio State University Press, 1974), 181-233.

11. In "The Idea of Romance in the Eighteenth-Century Novel," *Papers of the Michigan Academy of Sciences, Arts, and Letters* 49 (1964): 507-22, Sheridan Baker argues that eighteenth-century life was permeated with attitudes inherited from romances, such as the central daydream of success and the idea of excellence in conduct. Two studies by Henry Knight Miller also address the question of romance in eighteenth-century prose fiction. In "Augustan Prose Fiction and the Romance Tradition," *Studies in the Eighteenth Century,* ed. R. F. Brissenden and J. C. Eade (Toronto: University of Toronto Press, 1976), Miller argues that despite the rise of the novel, eighteenth-century novelists still followed the structures, patterns, motifs, and modes of characterization found in romance. He constructs a theoretical model for romance which he applies more specifically to one work, in his *Henry Fielding's Tom Jones and the Romance Tradition,* ELS Monograph Series, no. 6 (Victoria: University of Victoria Press, 1976). Recently, Jerry C. Beasley has published a somewhat modified version

of his 1976 article, "Romance and the 'New' Novels of Richardson, Fielding, and Smollett," in *Novels of the 1740's* (Athens: University of Georgia Press, 1982), 23-42.

For a more comprehensive theoretical discussion of the romance tradition and its relationship to other narrative traditions, see Scholes's and Kellogg's *The Nature of Narrative* and Northrop Frye's *The Secular Scripture* (Cambridge: Harvard University Press, 1976).

12. In *The Secular Scripture,* Northrop Frye discusses how the heroine of the *Aethiopica* and the stress on her virginity in that novel illustrate a romance displacement of the cycle of nature: "The heroine who becomes a bride, and eventually, one assumes, a mother on the last page of a romance, has accommodated herself to the cyclical movement: by her marriage, or whatever it is, she completes the cycle and passes out of the story" (80).

13. Clara Reeve, *The Progress of Romance* (1785; reprint, New York: Garland), 1:111.

14. Miller, "Augustan Prose Fiction," 252.

15. Miguel de Cervantes Saavedra, *The History of the Renowned Don Quixote,* trans. Peter Motteux (London, 1700), 585-86.

16. Ibid., 586.

17. Ibid., 583-84.

18. Ibid., 585.

19. In "Henry Fielding's Comic Epic-in-Prose Romances Again," *Philological Quarterly* 58 (1979): 63-81, Sheridan Baker rejects the notion that Fielding is following the epic tradition, except in occasional and peripheral instances of the mock-heroic. He suggests, instead, that "Fielding did not aim to write a modern epic; he aimed at something new: making Cervantic comedy out of realism and romance in native English terms. The epic had been done, and remained available to modern writers only in those heroics he excluded from his epicenter" (68). Baker demonstrates convincingly that Fielding does not follow the Homeric and Vergilian tradition of the epic and is not greatly influenced by Fénelon's prose rendering of that tradition in the *Télémaque*. Fielding's use of the term *epic,* Baker argues, is neutral, signifying "narration" rather than the classical tradition. He cites as evidence for this the Canon of Toledo's use of the term in his discourse on romances, in which Cervantes once uses the term to mean "narration" and a second time to mean "chivalric romances" (73). While I agree with Baker's argument that Fielding's novels are more romance than epic, I would contend that Baker passes over a meaning of *epic* that is clearly implied in both Fielding's and Cervantes' works.

20. All quotations from *Joseph Andrews, Tom Jones,* and *Amelia* are from the Wesleyan University editions of these texts.

21. See Fielding's comments on *Amelia* in the *Covent-Garden Journal,* 28 January 1752.

Chapter 2. The Heliodoran Novel

1. Jacques Amyot, "Le Proësme du translateur," *L'Histoire Aethiopique de Heliodorus* (Paris, 1547), [i]. English translations of the preface are mine: "de ne conter indifferemment toutes sortes de fables à leur petitz enfants, de peur que leurs ames des le commencement ne s'abreuvent de folie . . . de ne s'amuser à lire sans jugement toutes sortes de livres fabuleux: de peur que leurs entendements ne s'acoustument petit à petit à aymer mensonge, & a se paistre de vanité."

2. Amyot, "Le Proësme," [ii]: "par exemples du passé s'instruyre aux afaires de avenir."

3. Amyot, "Le Proësme," [ii]: "Mais tout ainsi comme en la portraiture les tableux sont estimez les meilleurs, & plaisent plus aux yeux à ces cognoissants, qui representent mieux la verité du naturel, aussi entre celles fictions celles qui sont les moins esloignées de nature, & ou il y a plus de verisimilitude, sont celles qui plaisent le plus à ceux qui mesurent leur plaisir à la raison, & qui se delectent avecq' jugement."

4. Amyot, "Le Proësme," [ii]: "n'est pas besoing que toutes choses y soient faintes, atendu que celà n'est point permis aux Poëtes mesmes."

5. Amyot, "Le Proësme," [ii]: Premierement en histoire, de laquelle la fin est verité. A raison dequoy il n'est point loysible aux Poëtes, quand ilz parlent des choses qui sont en nature d'en escrire à leur plaisir autrement que la verité n'est: pource que celà leur seroit imputé, non à licence, ou artifice: mais à ignorance. Secondement en ordre, & disposition, dont la fin est l'expression, & la force d'atraire & retinir le lecteur. Tiercement en la fiction, dont la fin est l'esbahissement, & la delectation, qui procede de la nouvelleté des chose estranges, & pleines de merveilles."

6. Amyot, "Le Proësme," [ii]: "se doit-on permettre toutes chose e[n] fictions que l'on veult desguiser du nom d'historiale verité: ains y fault entrelasser si dextrement du vray parmy du faux, en retenant tousjours semblance de verité, & si bien r'aporter le tout ensemble, qu'il n'y ayt point de discordance du commencement au mylieu, ny du mylieu à la fin."

7. Amyot, "Le Proësme," [ii- iii]: "si mal cousuz & si esloignez de toute vraysemblable aparence, qu'il semble que ce soient plus tost songes de quelque malade resuant en fièvre chaude, qu'inventions d'aucun homme d'esprit, & de jugement. Et pource m'est il avis qu'ilz ne sçavroient avoir la grace, ny la force de delecter le loysir d'un bon entendement: car ilz ne sont point dignes de luy. Et est un certain signe que celuy n'a point de sentiment des choses ingenieuses, & gentiles, qui se delecte des lourdes & grossieres."

8. Amyot, "Le Proësme," [iii]: "avecq' si grande honnesteté, qu l'on n'en sçavroit tirer ocasion, ou exemple de mal faire."

9. Amyot, "Le Proësme," [iii]: "il commence au mylieu de son histoire, comme sont les Poëtes Heroïques. Ce qui cause de prime face un grand esbahissement aux lecteurs, & leurs engendre un passioné desir d'entendre le commencement: & toutes fois il les tire si bien par l'ingenieuse liaison de son conte, qu'l'on n'est point resolu de ce que l'on trouve tout au commencement du premier livre jusques à ce que l'on ayt leu la fin du cinquieme. Et quand on en est là venu, encore a l'on plus grande envie de voir la fin, que l'on n'avoit au paravant d'en voir le commencement: De sorte que tousjours l'entendement demeure suspendu, jusques à ce que l'on viennent à la conclusion, laquelle laisse le lecteur satisfait, de la sorte que le sont ceux, qui à la fin viennent à jouyr d'un bien ardemment desiré, & longuement atendu."

10. Pierre-Daniel Huet, *Lettre- Traité sur l'Origine des Romans,* ed. Fabienne Gégou (Paris: Editions Nizet, 1971), 138. Translations mine: "amas de fictions grossièrement entassées les unes sur les autres."

11. Huet, *Lettre-Traité*, 47-48: "Les romans son plus simples, moins élevés et moins figurés dans l'invention et dans l'expression; les poèmes ont plus du merveilleux quoique toujours vraisemblables; les romans ont plus de vraisemblable quoiqu'ils aient quelquefois du merveilleux; les poèmes sont plus réglés et plus châtiés dans l'ordonnance et reçoivent moins de matière, d'événements et d'épisodes; les romans en reçoivent davantage parce qu'étant moins élevés et moins figurés, ils ne tendent

pas tant l'esprit et le laissent en état de se charger d'un plus grand nombre de différentes idées; enfin les poèmes ont pour sujet une action militaire ou politique et ne traitent l'amour que par occasion; les romans au contraire ont l'amour pour sujet principal et ne traitent le politique et la guerre que par incident."

12. Huet, *Lettre-Traité*, 78: "on y remarque beaucoup de fertilité et d'invention: les événements y sont fréquent, nouveaux, vraisemblables, bien arrangés, bien débrouillés; le dénouement en est admirable: il est naturel, il naît du sujet et rien n'est plus touchant ni plus pathétique."

13. Georges de Scudéry, "Preface to *Ibrahim*," trans. Henry Cogan, in *Prefaces to Fiction*, Augustan Reprint Society Publications, no. 32 (1952; reprint, New York: Kraus Reprint, 1967), 1. All further references to the preface will be cited internally.

14. For a discussion of decorum in the heroic novels, see Moses Ratner, *Theory and Criticism of the Novel in France from L'Astrée to 1740* (1938; reprint, New York: Russell, 1971), 27-30.

15. Heliodorus, *An Aethiopian History*, trans. Thomas Underdowne (1895; reprint, New York: AMS Press, 1967). All further references to this 1587 translation will be cited internally.

16. Madeleine de Scudéry, *Ibrahim, or the Illustrious Bassa*, trans. Henry Cogan (London, 1674), 69. All further references to the novel will be cited internally.

17. Amyot, "Le Proësme," [iii- iv].

18. Forcione, *Cervantes' Christian Romance*, 127.

Chapter 3. *Scarron's* Roman Comique

1. English Showalter, Jr. traces the development of realism in the late seventeenth- and early eighteenth- century French novels in *The Evolution of the French Novel: 1641-1782* (Princeton: Princeton University Press, 1972). He demonstrates that a new aesthetic of prose fiction—in which realism itself became an art form and in which fiction confesses itself to be fiction—developed after the demise of the heroic novels. He traces this development by considering five elements of prose fiction—time, place, names, money, and the narrator—that show more realistic forms of prose fiction departing from the epic and romance conventions of the mid-seventeenth-century novel. Showalter's study, although principally concerned with the French novel, offers a valuable perspective lacking in Ian Watt's *The Rise of the Novel*, in which sociological, economic, and philosophical factors are privileged and the continuous development of narrative conventions largely ignored.

2. Antoine Adam, ed., *Romanciers du dix-septième siècle* (Tours: Editions Gallimard, 1962), 38. See also Henri Coulet, *Le Roman jusqu'à la révolution*, (Paris: Armand Colin, 1967), 202; Joan De Jean, *Scarron's Roman Comique: A Comedy of the Novel, A Novel of Comedy* (Bern: Peter Lang, 1977), 65.

3. Sheridan Baker, "Henry Fielding's Comic Romances," *Papers of the Michigan Academy of Arts, Sciences, and Letters* 45 (1960): 413-14; Benjamin Boyce, ed., *The Comical Romance* (New York: Blom, 1968), xvii-xxii; Homer Goldberg, *The Art of Joseph Andrews* (Chicago: University of Chicago Press, 1969), 43-53.

4. Paul Scarron, *The Whole Comical Works of Monsr. Scarron*, introduction by Josephine Grieder (New York: Garland, 1973), 1:8. All further references to this reprint of Thomas Brown's 1700 translation of the *Roman Comique* will be cited internally.

5. The jeweled box is mentioned here and again when it is discovered that La Rappinière, one of the players' hosts in Mans, had stolen it. It does not reemerge

in the third part done by Offray, however, which perhaps indicates that Offray was not conscious of the potential implied by its presence here, or he did not choose to use the convention. Nevertheless, Scarron seems aware of the suspense such a device evokes.

6. De Jean notes that this opening periphrasis could be a parody of the opening of several chapters in Gomberville's *La Cytherée,* but that it is more generally a parody of the types of cliche' used frequently in the "high" style of heroic romances (37). Scarron's technique is to deflate conventional expectations by his unconventionally realistic voice. The method, as De Jean notes, is similar to using the heroic-novel convention as a "straight man" about to be the butt of a joke (39).

7. De Jean, *Scarron's Roman Comique,* 14.

8. See, for instance, the ending of *Tom Jones,* 7.4, where the narrator comments on Squire Western's jealousy toward Sophia for her loving his deceased wife as much as he hated her: "Which Sentiment being a pretty hard Morsel, and bearing Something of an Air of a Paradox, we shall leave the Reader to chew the Cud upon it to the End of the Chapter" (*Tom Jones,* 340).

Chapter 4. Joseph Andrews

1. It is commonplace in Fielding criticism to see a change in *Joseph Andrews* after the *Pamela* burlesque with which the novel opens. Among the numerous studies that cite this change are: Aurelien Digeon, *The Novels of Henry Fielding* (1925; reprint, New York: Russell, 1962), 53; H. K. Banerji, *Henry Fielding* (1929; reprint, New York: Russell, 1962), 125; Andrew Wright, *Henry Fielding: Mask and Feast* (Berkeley: University of California Press, 1966), 57. Robert Alan Donovan, in "*Joseph Andrews* as Parody," in *The Shaping Vision: Imagination in the Novel from Defoe to Dickens* (Ithaca: Cornell University Press, 1966), 68-88, notes the shift from the *Pamela* burlesque in the middle section of the novel and the return to it at the end, but argues that the novel as a whole sustains a criticism of Richardson's novel. See also Martin C. Battestin, "Introduction," *Joseph Andrews and Shamela* (Boston: Houghton Mifflin, 1961), xviii.

Discussions of the Cervantine manner in *Joseph Andrews* are numerous. For one challenging view that attempts to make sense of the shift in directions in terms of Fielding's indebtedness to Cervantes, see Maurice Johnson, *Fielding's Art of Fiction* (Philadelphia: University of Pennsylvania Press, 1961), 47-49. Johnson compares the shift from *Pamela* to the romance story of Joseph and Fanny to the change in direction that Cervantes takes in *Don Quixote*—the shift from a satire on chivalric romances to a "good" romance concerned with society and character.

2. Amyot, "Le Proësme," [iii].

3. Fielding makes it clear in the prefatory chapter to book 3 of *Joseph Andrews* that *history* means to him not mere narration of facts, but portrayals of humankind: "I describe not Men but Manners; not an Individual but a Species" (189). In 2.1 of *Tom Jones,* Fielding comments on the kind of selectivity and emphasis that governs his "new Province of Writing:"

> Whenever any extraordinary Scene presents itself (as we trust will often be the Case) we shall spare no Pains nor Paper to open it at large to our Reader; but if whole Years should pass without producing any thing worthy of his Notice, we shall not be afraid of a Chasm in our History; but shall hasten on to Matters of Consequence, and leave such Periods of time totally unobserved. (*Tom Jones,* 76)

Leo Braudy, in *Narrative Form in History and Fiction* (Princeton: Princeton University Press, 1970), sees Fielding's historical procedure as creating a fictional world that helps us understand the actual: "By using facts in *Joseph Andrews* to make particular points or complete specific causal progressions, Fielding implies that individual facts in fiction and history should be used only in a frame of causal or circumstantial relevance" (110). See also Philip Stevick, "Fielding and the Meaning of History," *PMLA* 79 (1964): 561-68; John J. Burke, Jr., "History without History: Fielding's Theory of Fiction," in *A Provision of Human Nature*, ed. Donald Kay (University: University of Alabama Press, 1977), 45-63.

4. In *The Rise of the Novel*, Ian Watt defines "formal realism" as follows: "the premise, or primary convention, that the novel is a full and authentic report of human experience, and is therefore under an obligation to satisfy its readers with such details of the story as the individuality of the actors concerned, the particulars of the times and places of their actions, details of which are presented through a more largely referential use of language than is common in other literary forms" (22).

5. In part 1 of the *Cyrus*, while Artamène is fighting on behalf of King Cyaxare, Mandane's father and the hero's mortal enemy, the hero is reported dead—a fact that confirms for the heroine her then unacknowledged love for the hero.

6. The incident of Fanny's attack in the woods, significantly enough, follows Adams's conversation with a gentleman about heroic bravery; when the pair hear Fanny's shrieks, the gentleman, who has disinherited a nephew for refusing a commission in the West Indies, departs, while Adams goes to Fanny's aid. The battle between Adams and the ravisher takes on the appearance of a mock-heroic struggle— a choice which emphasizes both the romance potential of the scene and the baseness of the ravisher, who later accuses Fanny of being a whore and Adams of being a robber. Adams, in his quixotic way, however, plays the role of a romance champion and, more important, of an agent of providence (see especially 2.9, *Joseph Andrews*, 129).

In 2.10, before Adams and Fanny are taken before the justice, Fanny herself entertains notions of a romance plight:

> She began to fear as great an Enemy in her Deliverer, as he had delivered her from; and as she had not Light enough to discover the Age of Adams, and the Benevolence visible in his Countenance, she suspected he had used her as some very honest Men have used their Country; and had rescued her out of the Hands of one Rifler, in order to rifle her himself. (*Joseph Andrews*, 140)

Fanny's momentary fear pinpoints exactly the dilemma of a Heliodoran novel heroine when she is captured by one villain and rescued by another, more villainous one. The irony here is that Fielding's narrative perspective allows us to see Adams's benevolent motives without the physical light that in the causal-similar situation prevents Fanny from recognizing her old friend. The result is a suggestion of romance convention that momentarily halts the causal-similar logic and thereby emphasizes the romance quality of the scene.

7. The accidents precipitated by the trio's impecunity, on one level, accord with the causal-similar movement of the plot. In 2.13, in fact, Fielding even presents an itemized account of their finances (*Joseph Andrews*, 161). The fact of their poverty emphasizes not only the hypocrisy and greed of characters such as Parson Trulliber and the promising "squire," but also the generosity and humility of characters such as the peddler and Mr. Wilson.

On a symbolic level, however, the financial distresses of the trio set up a pattern similar to that of Cervantes in the *Persiles*. In traveling through the Northern seas to Europe, Periandro and Auristela move from one "haven" to another, where they typically discover immediate succor but more imminent danger. By this narrative frame, Cervantes is able to diversify the unified plot line. At the haven, the hero and heroine meet with characters whose stories reflect or contrast with the dilemmas of the hero and heroine. The result is a multi-webbed plot line that, though episodic at times, is deeply textured. Initially, Fielding's strategy does not seem so deeply textured; we assume, for instance, that once the episodes of the peddler and Mr. Wilson are over, these characters will not reappear, just as Trulliber and the promising "squire" do not reappear. When it turns out that both the peddler and Wilson are important to the resolution of the novel, it becomes clear that the novel is not so episodic as it seems to be.

8. In many respects the episode at Wilson's secluded home structurally resembles the function of the hermitage of Renato and Eusebia at the end of book 2 of the *Persiles*. Just as the Wilson episode occurs approximately halfway through the journey of Adams, Joseph, and Fanny, the episode at Renato's occurs exactly halfway through the *Persiles*. Renato and Eusebia receive the travelers with good will, as do Wilson and his wife, even though they are strangers. Although in the middle of a barbarous sea, Renato's hermitage displays vestiges of the "true" religion: they have an altar with images of Christ, the Blessed Virgin, and John. At Wilson's, Joseph and company receive the kind of Christian charity that they have found lacking in the outside world.

Wilson's house is marked by its simplicity and its lack of ostentation, just as Renato's is "fitter to lead a poore life therein, than to rejoyce with any superfluity" (*Persiles*, 199). In addition, Renato's hermitage sems to have an Edenic air about it; it was

> so full of trees bearing fruit, so fresh by reason of the waters wherewith it was every where moistened, so delightful for the verdure of the grasse, and so sweet and faire with diversitie of flowers, that at one time in the same degree it was able to content the five senses. (*Persiles*, 200)

Similarly, Wilson's garden seems to invoke an Edenic quality:

> No Parterres, no Fountains, no Statues embellished this little Garden. Its only Ornament was a short Walk, shaded on each side by a Filbert Hedge, with a small Alcove at one end, whither in hot Weather the Gentleman and his Wife used to retire and divert themselves with their Children, who played in the Walk before them: But tho' Vanity had no Votary in this little Spot, here was variety of Fruit, and every thing useful for the Kitchin. (*Joseph Andrews*, 226)

Just as the hermitage in Cervantes' novel provides a sort of retreat where true religious piety can grow, so Wilson's house provides a retreat from the ostentation of the outside world—a place where innocence and goodness can grow.

The parallel between the two scenes is incidental, of course; Fielding does not model his digression after Cervantes', but it is useful to note that in both cases, the "havens" serve important thematic functions. Both are Edenic retreats from the barbarism of the civilized world; both episodes provide momentary glimpses of thematic hope: in the *Persiles*, the survival of true religion; in *Joseph Andrews*, the survival of true Christian charity. Both episodes, though apparently thematic digressions, play important parts in the final revelation of the hero's and heroine's identities. Rutilio replaces Renato at the hermitage and thus accidently prepares the way for Seráfido to find Periandro at the end of the novel. Wilson tells Adams of his stolen son with the strawberry birthmark, thus providing the key to Joseph's identity.

9. Joseph's rhetorical lament in 3.11 is analogous to the conventional response of heroes in the Heliodoran tradition to the apparent loss of their loves. Although Joseph's reaction is conventional, Fielding places rhetorical emphasis on Adams's sermon about a stoically Christian submission to providence. What is curious here is that Fielding uses Adams's long-winded response as a substitute for the conventional complaints. As I have noted earlier, when Justinian in the *Ibrahim* is separated from Isabelle and captured by Soliman, he laments the designs of providence but resolves stoically to accept whatever fortune brings him. Here Adams's sermon emphasizes the submission to providence while Joseph's lament emphasizes his feelings.

10. Lady Booby's plot with Lawyer Scout (4.3) to have Fanny arrested, and her indirect collusion with Beau Didapper's plan to steal Fanny away (4.13), cast Lady Booby in a role analogous to Arsace and Hipólita. All three are infatuated with the heroes and use their wealth and power to try to get rid of the heroines. Both of Lady Bellaston's plots are unsuccessful, but they play important roles in producing the penultimate complications that seem to make the hero's and heroine's marriage, now that they are reunited, seem impossible.

11. Henry Fielding, *Jonathan Wild,* vol. 2 of *The Complete Works of Henry Fielding,* ed. William E. Henley (1903; reprint, New York: Barnes and Noble, 1967), 188.

Chapter 5. Tom Jones

1. Henry Knight Miller, in *Tom Jones and the Romance Tradition,* offers the most sustained analysis of the romance patterns in the novel. He argues that, although Fielding occasionally parodies individual elements of romance, his novels are not essentially parodic: "Fielding could still vitally and integrally employ the structures and the motifs of romance in his own comic mode because he still whole-heartedly believed . . . in the fundamental cosmic, metaphysical, and social assumptions that had for so long sustained the romance" (20-21). Given this view, Miller defines the tripartite structure of *Tom Jones* in terms of the archetypal pattern of Departure (Exile), Initiation, and Return. Even though Fielding's setting gives prominence to actuality of time and space, Miller argues that it nevertheless emphasizes the timeless and spaceless qualities of romance. Characters embrace both the typological world of romance and the individual world of novelistic realism.

Critics who recognize the causal pattern of history in the novel include Philip Stevick who, in "Fielding and the Meaning of History," argues that Fielding's romance tendency is an escape from history, but also that his novels are

> at once romances and antiromances; the romance elements are assimilated into a form which is concretely of the author's time and place, and indeed the very legitimacy of the romance elements is often tested by comparison with a fictional milieu which is critically historical. There is, finally, little impulse to simplify and little impulse to escape. (567)

Leo Braudy, in *Narrative Forms in History and Fiction,* notes that Fielding creates a tension between his historical pose and his romanticizing of certain elements. This tension, along with others, creates a narrative pose in which history is not the "ironclad" pattern of causality in which effect necessarily proceeds from cause, but the means of retrospectively explaining the pattern of history:

Coincidence in *Tom Jones* emphasizes the control of the narrator and attunes the reader to the often strange concatenations of events that he may expect from life. By producing the necessary explanation only *after* the effect has been achieved and the scene witnessed, the narrator reveals that the elaborate patterns we make of history are only retrospectively ironclad and knowable. (167)

2. In "The Plot of *Tom Jones*," in *Tom Jones*, ed. Sheridan Baker (New York: Norton, 1973), R. S. Crane notes that the consequences of Tom's imprudence create in the reader "a kind of faint alarm which is the comic analogue of fear" (863). We momentarily expect a calamity for Jones, but it is momentary because Fielding prompts us to "instinctively infer from past occurrences . . . what will probably happen next or in the end, and what steadily cumulates in this way, in spite of the gradual worsening of Tom's situation, is an opinion that, since nothing irreparable has so far happened to him, nothing ever will" (866). A similar pattern occurs in a romance structure, such as the Heliodoran novel, which is not guided by a comic manner: we instinctively believe in the providential scheme of events, even though incidents at any given point make us doubt that scheme.

3. In the prefatory chapter to book 15, for instance, Fielding calls our attention to the issue of providence and the nature of poetic justice by ironically arguing against the notion that "Virtue is the certain Road to Happiness, and Vice to Misery in this World" (*Tom Jones*, 783). If virtue means "pursuing the Good of others as [one's] own," it often produces "Backbiting, Envy, and Ingratitude" (*Tom Jones*, 783-84). Fielding finally dismisses the doctrine as untrue and un-Christian. It does not produce happiness in this world (as is evident by the way people treat the virtuous), but in the next. Although ironically posed, the argument reinforces a fundamentally romance belief in providence: despite apparent earthly injustice, virtue *will* ultimately be rewarded. Tom's eventual reward, especially coming from characters named Allworthy and Sophia, suggests the otherworldly operation of this principle.

4. Cyrus is the victim of false rumors when Mandane suspects that he was unfaithful to her with Princess Araminte. The confusion stems both from Artamène's resemblance to Prince Spithridates, Araminte's actual lover, and from the machinations of the King of Pontus (one of Artamène's rivals for Mandane), who shows the hero a letter from Araminte, his sister.

5. The conventions of the picaresque never really apply to *Tom Jones*, if we accept Claudio Guillén's characteristics of that form in *Literature as System: Essays Toward a Theory of Literary History* (Princeton: Princeton University Press, 1971), 75-84. He describes the picaresque as the narrative of a wandering, introspective hero, the form of which is determined by his being an outcast. The *pícaro's* reflections, partial and prejudiced as they are, influence the form. English Showalter, Jr., in *The Evolution of the French Novel*, however, demonstrates that the particular struggles that a *pícaro* faces—the exigencies of money, for example—play a considerable role in the evolution of realism in the eighteenth-century novel (75). In a restrictive sense of the picaresque, the two elements of Tom's character that most resemble that of the *pícaro* are: (1) his wandering, seemingly in an aimless fashion, and (2) the consequences of his material survival, such as his reliance on Lady Bellaston's money in the London section. Both of these create something of the panoramic, satiric view of life that is common in eighteenth-century picaresque novels, such as Lesage's *Gil Blas* and Smollett's *Roderick Random*.

6. When Mrs. Fitzpatrick tries to seduce Tom, Tom responds with a "Profession of generous Sentiments" that the Narrator says "would have become the Mouth

of Oroondates himself" (*Tom Jones*, 870). The allusion, to La Calprenède's *Cassandre*, had become a cliché in the eigthteenth century.

7. The film of *Tom Jones*, written by John Osborne and directed by Tony Richardson, is perhaps the best example of the glorification of Tom's sexual roguishness. See Martin C. Battestin, "Osborne's *Tom Jones*: Adapting a Classic," *Virginia Quarterly Review* 42 (1966): 378-93. Closer to Fielding's time, Samuel Johnson's remarks in the *Rambler* essay (31 March 1750) catch the flavor of Tom's appearance as a splendidly wicked hero. For other contemporary reactions to Tom's immoral behavior, see Frederic T. Blanchard's *Fielding the Novelist* (1926; reprint, New York: Russell, 1966), 49-70.

8. In Tom's sexual escapades with Mrs. Waters and Lady Bellaston, Fielding consciously brings up the issue of hunger; indeed, it almost serves as a *leitmotif* that reinforces the distinction the author draws between benevolent love and sexual hunger. The "battle of the amorous Kind" in 9.5 is preceded by a philosophical commentary on the necessity of eating, even for the "greatest Prince, Heroe, or Philosopher" (*Tom Jones*, 509). When Mrs. Waters launches her assault, Tom is momentarily preserved by the "God of Eating." The narrator comments on the ironic inversion of the romance cliché: "For as Love frequently preserves from the Attacks of Hunger, so may Hunger possibly, in some Cases, defend us against Love" (*Tom Jones*, 512). Later the narrator attributes the episode to Mrs. Waters's sexual appetite: "The Beauty of Jones highly charmed her Eye; but as she could not see his Heart, she gave herself no concern about it. She could feast heartily at the Table of Love, without reflecting that some other already had been, or hereafter might be, feasted with the same Repast" (*Tom Jones*, 518).

Just before Tom goes to the masquerade in book 13 where he meets Lady Bellaston, the narrator describes his situation once again in terms of the love-hunger conflict:

> Now if the Antient Opinion, that Men might live very comfortably on Virtue only, be . . . a notorious Error; no less false is, I apprehend, that Position of some Writers of Romance, that a man can live altogether on Love: For however delicious Repasts this may afford to some of our Senses or Appetites, it is most certain it can afford none to others. Those, therefore, who have placed too great Confidence in such Writers, have experienced their Error when it was too late; and have found that Love was no more capable of delighting the Ear, or a Violin of gratifying the Smell. (*Tom Jones*, 710)

The reduction to absurdity here clearly parallels the reductive technique of Fielding's assault on ill-natured philosophers in 10.1, but it also sets up an important distinction. One should not confuse sensual hunger with love, nor love with the food that satisfies sensual hunger.

9. Fielding's use of the analogy from Locke's *Essay Concerning Human Understanding* points out a similarity between Fielding's philosophical view of benevolent love and the "moral sense" philosophers, such as Francis Hutcheson. These philosophers, deriving their system from Locke's epistemology, argue that the "moral sense" exists as a separate faculty, analogous to the five senses, which prompts our approval or disapproval of moral actions. Like Fielding's notion of "good-nature" in his *Essay on the Knowledge of the Characters of Men*, Hutcheson believes that the moral sense is separate from reason. Reason corrects its impressions when our moral sense is impaired in some way, just as reason corrects the external senses when its faculties are impaired. See Francis Hutcheson, *Illustrations on the Moral Sense* (Cambridge: Harvard University Press, 1971), 163. What Fielding argues for here is the ability of a reader,

whose heart is operating without impairment, to see how the ill- natured readers' hearts are impaired.

10. Partridge serves as an agent largely because he informs both Tom and Allworthy of Mrs. Waters's identity. Notably, Partridge is also a guide whose knowledge of Tom's identity throughout is incomplete. In this sense, he is analogous to the companions of the hero and heroine in the Heliodoran novel who suspect that the hero and heroine are greater than they are.

11. The confusion of Sophia with Jenny Cameron signals an intersection of Fielding's fictional history with actual historical events. Braudy points out that the incident has "little 'reality' or 'meaning' beyond that imposed upon it by characters for their own interests" (177). Indeed, the landlord in 11.2 who thinks Sophia is one of the Young Pretender's mistresses bears this theory out. The landlord was "thought to see farther and deeper into Things than any Man in the Parish" (*Tom Jones*, 576) and thus sees Sophia as an opportunity both to lord his opinions over his wife and to gain an interest at court should the rebellion succeed. On another level, however, the mistaken identity follows a pattern of confusion that is consistent with Fielding's displacement of romance conventions elsewhere. Just as Joseph, Fanny, and Tom are thought, at times, to be nobler than they are because they convey an air of gentility, so the landlord interprets Sophia's humble behavior as a kind of *noblesse oblige*. Although our knowledge of the reality of Sophia's identity—like our knowledge of Tom's, Joseph's, and Fanny's—prevents our falling into the same trap as the landlord, what emerges is a portrait of Sophia's inner nobility that cannot be hidden despite her appearance, just as Chariclea's and Auristela's real qualities cannot be hidden by their assumed disguises.

12. Beasley observes in *Novels of the 1740s* that "Fielding subjects his characters to accidents and threats which test them, but in the end, as benevolent manipulator, he procures for them the good they deserve" (193). Beasley argues that Fielding's self-conscious role as artist in all of his novels serves to reinforce his reader's belief in the design of Providence.

13. John Preston, in *The Created Self: The Reader's Role in Eighteenth-Century Fiction* (London: Heinemann, 1970), argues that *Tom Jones* is a "structure of successive responses to the novel" whose effect is "epistemological rather than moral" (114). Wolfgang Iser's "The Role of the Reader in Fielding's *Joseph Andrews* and *Tom Jones*," in his *The Implied Reader* (Baltimore: Johns Hopkins University Press, 1974), argues that Fielding's narrator stimulates "a process of learning in the course of which one's own sense of judgment may come under scrutiny" (31). He describes two principal methods by which Fielding leaves gaps in the text: "schematized views" (the same event viewed from different aspects) and the "principle of contrast" (the presentations of characters, such as Sophia and Molly, who embody contrasting moral values). Both techniques create vacant spaces in the text that invite the reader "to enter into the proceedings in such a way that he can construct their meaning" (51).

Chapter 6. Amelia

1. Henry Fielding, *The Covent-Garden Journal* (1915; reprint, New York: Russell, 1964), 1:186.

2. See Lyall Powers, "The Influence of the *Aeneid* on Fielding's *Amelia*," *MLN* 71 (1956): 330-36; Maurice Johnson, "The Noble Model," in *Fielding's Art of Fiction*, 139-56; Robert Alter, "Fielding's Problem Novel," in *Fielding and the Nature of the Novel* (Cambridge: Harvard University Press, 1968), 144-48.

3. Sheridan Baker, in "Fielding's *Amelia* and the Materials of Romance," *Philological Quarterly* 41 (1962): 437-49, points out correspondences between specific incidents in *Amelia*—such as the wine-hamper episode, the masquerade, and the character of Atkinson—and the tradition of romance. He argues that instead of keeping romance devices at an "amused distance" as he did in *Tom Jones* and *Joseph Andrews*, Fielding uses the romance devices in *Amelia* for a serious purpose. As a result, the novel "falters at the very places where he has attempted to use the old romantic devices that his old comic viewpoint had made viable" (447-48).

Other critics find the novel dissatisfying for different reasons. Andrew Wright, for example, in *Henry Fielding: Mask and Feast*, sees the structure as "anything but successful," attributing the failure to "the number and quality of static and detached discussions of topics whose relationship to the main course of action is tenuous at best" (106-7). Other critics regard it as too blatantly moralistic: see Frederic Karl, "A Note on *Amelia*," in *Reader's Guide to the Eighteenth-Century Novel* (New York: Noonday, 1974), 179-82; Eustace Palmer, "*Amelia*—The Decline of Fielding's Art," *Essays in Criticism* 21 (1971): 135-51.

Leo Braudy, in *Narrative Form in History and Fiction*, notes the flaws in the novel but gives it a more important role in Fielding's exploration of history: "Perhaps one reason for the relative failure of *Amelia* is that Fielding wishes to build a firmer link to the real world of action, and the novel suffers the strain. *Amelia* is as much a creation as *Tom Jones*, but less self-contained in its implications. In his last novel Fielding experiments with the relation between the private world of the individual and the public world of society, between the private world of a work of art and the actuality on which it is based and to which it must refer" (183).

4. The destruction of Amelia's nose is one the reasons why Fielding's imaginary critics in the *Covent- Garden Journal*'s "Court of Censorial Enquiry" (25 January 1752) condemn the novel. For an account of the controversy, see Blanchard's *Fielding the Novelist*, 85-90. Although the breaking of her nose is a "historical" accident, Booth makes it clear in his narration that the loss of her nose's beauty defines a kind of heroism on Amelia's part:

> What a Maganimity of Mind did her Behaviour demonstrate! If the World have extolled the Firmness of Soul in a Man who can support the Loss of Fortune; of a General, who can be composed after the loss of a Victory; of a King, who can be contented with the Loss of a Crown; with what Astonishment ought we to behold, with what Praises to honour a young Lady, who can with Patience and Resignation submit to the Loss of exquisite Beauty, in other Words to the Loss of Fortune, Power, Glory; every Thing which human Nature is apt to court and rejoice in! What must be the Mind, which can bear to be deprived of all these in a Moment, and by an unfortunate trifling Accident. (*Amelia*, 67)

Booth's making much of the trivial incident defines his susceptibility to sentimental effusion. But it also suggests a displacement of the kind of lavish embellishment that occurs when heroes and heroines in the Heliodoran novel are subjected to the accidents of fortune.

5. See Baker's "*Amelia* and the Materials of Romance," 437-38.

6. Ibid., 439.

7. Curiously, when Amelia, attired only in her dressing gown, visits Booth at the bailiff's in 12.2, the bailiff's wife thinks the heroine a prostitute. This incident clearly shows the opposite of the romance convention: the gentle, chaste heroine's inner nobility does not outshine the mask of reality.

8. Amelia, like Isabelle, follows the hero on his military expedition without his knowledge or his prompting her. Her reason for going, much like Fanny's in *Joseph Andrews,* is a rumor that Booth has been mortally injured. Fielding casts her decision in a romance light by giving Amelia's explanation a hyperbolic quality: "O Mr. Booth! and do you know so little of your Amelia, as to think I could or would survive you!—Would it not be better for one dreadful Sight to break my Heart at once, than to break it by Degrees?" (*Amelia*, 117).

9. Like Amelia, Mrs. Bennet came under the lord's power when he and her husband lived in the verge at Mrs. Ellison's. The lord pretended a friendship both by his affections toward their son and by a promise to help Mr. Bennet regain the living that he had been cheated of. While Mr. Bennet is away on a futile trip (set up by the lord) to talk with his bishop, the peer takes Mrs. Bennet to a masquerade, drugs her, and rapes her. When her husband discovers her infidelity (Mrs. Bennet contracted syphilis from the lord), he is given over to such a rage that he dies of a heart attack. Mrs. Bennet's recital recalls the recitals of the Heliodoran novel tradition not only in its intrusive length, but also in its didactic purpose. Like the interpolated histories in the *Persiles,* Mrs. Bennet's history clearly points out dangers that Amelia and Booth should avoid.

10. In the *Aethiopica,* Chariclea pretends to agree to Thyamis's proposal of marriage in order to protect herself and the hero. Similarly, Auristela pretends to accede to Prince Arnaldo's overtures. Amelia's situation is different in that James's overtures are clearly illicit, but the danger to the hero is the same. Auristela's and Chariclea's actions keep Thyamis and Arnaldo in the status of friendly rivals—a position that James hypocritically feigns.

11. John Middleton Murry, for example, in "In Defense of Fielding," *Unprofessional Essays* (1956; reprint, Westport, Conn: Greenwood, 1975), sees the change in *Amelia* as the result of "growing physical exhaustion" (45).

Bibliography

Adam, Antoine, ed. *Romanciers du dix-septième siècle.* Tours: Editions Gallimard, 1962.

Alter, Robert. *Fielding and the Nature of the Novel.* Cambridge: Harvard University Press, 1968.

Amyot, Jacques. "Le Proësme du translateur." In *L'Histoire Aethiopique de Heliodorus.* Paris, 1547.

Aronson, Nicole. *Mademoiselle de Scudéry.* Translated by Stuart R. Aronson. Boston: Twayne, 1978.

Atkinson, William. "The Enigma of the *Persiles.*" *Bulletin of Hispanic Studies* 24 (1947): 242-53.

Baker, Ernest A. *The History of the English Novel.* Vol. 1. 1924. Reprint. New York: Barnes and Noble, 1950.

Baker, Sheridan. "*Amelia* and the Materials of Romance." *Philological Quarterly* 41 (1962): 437-49.

_____. "Henry Fielding's Comic Romances." *Papers of the Michigan Academy of Sciences, Arts, and Letters* 45 (1960): 411-19.

_____. "Fielding's Comic Epic-in-Prose Romances Again." *Philological Quarterly* 58 (1979): 63-81.

_____. "The Idea of Romance in the Eighteenth-Century Novel." *Papers of the Michigan Academy of Sciences, Arts, and Letters* 49 (1964): 507-22.

Banerji, H. K. *Henry Fielding.* 1929. Reprint. New York: Russell, 1962.

Barclay, John. *Argenis, or the Loves of Poliarchus and Argenis.* Translated by Kingsmill Long. London, 1625.

Battestin, Martin C. *The Moral Basis of Fielding's Art: A Study of Joseph Andrews.* Middletown, Conn.: Wesleyan University Press, 1959.

_____. "Osborne's *Tom Jones:* Adapting a Classic." *Virginia Quarterly Review* 42 (1966): 378-93.

Beasley, Jerry C. *Novels of the 1740s.* Athens: University of Georgia Press, 1982.

Bissel, Frederic O. *Fielding's Theory of the Novel.* 1933. Reprint. New York: Cooper Square, 1969.

Blanchard, Frederic T. *Fielding the Novelist: A Study in Historical Criticism.* 1926. Reprint. New York: Russell, 1966.

Booth, Wayne C. *The Rhetoric of Fiction.* Chicago: University of Chicago Press, 1961.

Braudy, Leo. *Narrative Form in History and Fiction: Hume, Fielding, and Gibbon.* Princeton: Princeton University Press, 1970.

Burke, John J., Jr. "History Without History: Fielding's Theory of Fiction." In *A Provision of Human Nature,* edited by Donald Kay, 45-63. University: University of Alabama Press, 1977.

Cervantes Saavedra, Miguel de. *The History of the Renowned Don Quixote.* Translated by Peter Motteux. London, 1700.

——————. *Novelas Ejemplares.* Vol. 1 of *Biblioteca de Autores Españoles.* Madrid, 1944.

——————. *Los Trabajos de Persiles y Sigismunda.* Edited by Juan Bautista Avalle-Arce. Madrid: Clasicos Castalia, 1969.

——————. *The Travels of Persiles and Sigismunda.* Translated from the Spanish. London, 1619.

Clark, A. F. B. *Jean Racine.* 1939. Reprint. New York: Octogon Books, 1969.

Congreve, William. *The Complete Works of William Congreve.* Edited by Montague Summers. 4 vols. 1914. Reprint. New York: Russell, 1924.

Cooke, Arthur L. "Henry Fielding and the Writers of Heroic Romance." *PMLA* 62 (1947): 984-94.

Coulet, Henri. *Le Roman jusqu'à la révolution.* Paris: Armand Colin, 1967.

Crane, R. S. "The Plot of *Tom Jones.*" In *Tom Jones,* edited by Sheridan Baker, 844-69. New York: Norton, 1973.

Davis, Walter R. *Idea and Act in Elizabethan Prose Fiction.* Princeton: Princeton University Press, 1969.

De Jean, Joan. *Scarron's Roman Comique: A Comedy of the Novel of Comedy.* Bern: Peter Lang, 1977.

Digeon, Aurelion. *The Novels of Henry Fielding.* 1925. Reprint. New York: Russell, 1962.

Donovan, Robert Alan. "*Joseph Andrews* as Parody." In *The Shaping Vision: Imagination in the Novel from Defoe to Dickens,* 68-88. Ithaca: Cornell University Press, 1966.

Fielding, Henry. *Amelia.* Edited by Martin C. Battestin. Middletown, Conn.: Wesleyan University Press, 1983.

——————. *The Covent-Garden Journal.* 2 vols. 1915. Reprint. New York: Russell, 1964.

——————. *The History of Tom Jones.* Edited by Fredson Bowers. Middletown, Conn.: Wesleyan University Press, 1975.

——————. *Jonathan Wild.* Vol. 2 of *The Complete Works of Henry Fielding,* edited by William E. Henley. 1903. Reprint. New York: Barnes and Noble, 1967.

_____. *Joseph Andrews*. Edited by Martin C. Battestin. Middletown, Conn.: Wesleyan University Press, 1967.

_____. *Joseph Andrews and Shamela*. Edited by Martin C. Battestin. Boston: Houghton Mifflin, 1961.

Forcione, Alban K. *Cervantes, Aristotle, and the Persiles*. Princeton: Princeton University Press, 1970.

_____. *Cervantes' Christian Romance: A Study of Persiles y Sigismunda*. Princeton: Princeton University Press, 1972.

Frye, Northrop. *The Secular Scripture: A Study of the Structure of Romance*. Cambridge: Harvard University Press, 1976.

Gabriel, Albinio Martín. "Heliodoro y la novela española." *Cuadernos de Literatura* 8 (1950): 215-34.

Goldberg, Homer. *The Art of Joseph Andrews*. Chicago: University of Chicago Press, 1969.

Guillén, Claudio. *Literature as System: Essays toward a Theory of Literary History*. Princeton: Princeton University Press, 1971.

Harrison, Bernard. *Henry Fielding's Tom Jones: The Novelist as Moral Philosopher*. Sussex: Sussex University Press, 1975.

Heiserman, Arthur. *The Novel Before the Novel*. Chicago: University of Chicago Press, 1977.

Heliodorus. *An Aethiopian History*. Translated by Thomas Underdowne. 1895. Reprint. New York: AMS Press, 1967.

_____. *The Aethiopian History of Heliodorus*. Translated by "A Person of Quality" and Nahum Tate. London, 1686.

Huet, Pierre-Daniel. *Lettre-Traité de Pierre-Daniel Huet sur l'origine des romans suivie de la Lecture des vieux romans par Jean Chapelain*. Edited by Fabienne Gégou. Paris: A.-G. Nizet, 1971.

Hunter, J. Paul. *Occasional Form: Henry Fielding and the Chains of Circumstance*. Baltimore: Johns Hopkins University Press, 1975.

Hutcheson, Francis. *Illustrations on the Moral Sense*. Edited by Bernard Peach. Cambridge: Harvard University Press, 1971.

Iser, Wolfgang. "The Role of the Reader in Fielding's *Joseph Andrews* and *Tom Jones*." In *The Implied Reader: Patterns of Communication in Prose Fiction from Bunyan to Beckett*, 29-56. Baltimore: Johns Hopkins University Press, 1974.

Johnson, Maurice. *Fielding's Art of Fiction: Essays on Shamela, Joseph Andrews, Tom Jones, and Amelia*. Philadelphia: University of Pennsylvania Press, 1961.

Karl, Frederic. *Reader's Guide to the Eighteenth- Century Novel*. New York: Noonday, 1974.

Kassier, Theodore L. *The Truth Disguised: Allegorical Structure and Technique in Gracián's El Criticón*. London: Tamesis, 1976.

Langford, Gerald. "John Barclay's *Argenis*: A Seminal Novel." *Studies in English* 26 (1947): 59-76.

Magendie, Maurice. *Le Roman français au dix-septième siècle: De L'Astrée au Grand Cyrus*. Paris: E. Droz, 1932.

Maresca, Thomas E. *Epic to Novel.* Columbus: Ohio State University Press, 1974.

Miller, Henry Knight. "Augustan Prose Fiction and the Romance Tradition." In *Studies in the Eighteenth Century,* edited by R. F. Brissenden and J. C. Eade. Toronto: University of Toronto Press, 1976.

_____. "The 'Digressive' Tales in Fielding's *Tom Jones* and the Perspective of Romance." *Philological Quarterly* 54 (1975): 258–74.

_____. *Henry Fielding's Tom Jones and the Romance Tradition.* ELS Monograph Series, no. 6. Victoria: University of Victoria Press, 1976.

Mish, Charles C., ed. *Short Fiction of the Seventeenth Century.* New York: New York University Press, 1963.

Morgan, Charlotte E. *The Rise of the Novel of Manners: A Study of English Prose Fiction Between 1600 and 1740.* 1939. Reprint. New York: Russell, 1963.

Munro, James S. "Richardson, Marivaux, and the Romance Tradition." *Modern Language Review* 70 (1975): 752–59.

Murry, John Middleton. "In Defense of Fielding." In *Unprofessional Essays,* 11–52. 1956. Reprint. Westport, Conn.: Greenwood Press, 1975.

Neill, Diana. *A Short History of the English Novel.* 1951. Reprint. New York: Collier, 1964.

Olsen, Flemming. "Notes on the Structure of *Joseph Andrews.*" *English Studies* 50 (1969): 340–51.

Palmer, Eustace. "*Amelia*: The Decline of Fielding's Art." *Essays in Criticism* 21 (1971): 135–51.

Perry, Ben Edwin. *The Ancient Romances: A Literary-Historical Account of Their Origin.* Berkeley: University of California Press, 1967.

Powers, Lyall. "The Influence of the *Aeneid* on Fielding's *Amelia.*" *Modern Language Notes* 71 (1956): 330–36.

Preston, John. *The Created Self: The Reader's Role in Eighteenth-Century Fiction.* London: Heinemann, 1970.

Ratner, Moses. *Theory and Criticism of the Novel in France from L'Astrée to 1740.* 1938. Reprint. New York: Russell, 1971.

Reeve, Clara. *The Progress of Romance through Times, Countries, and Manners.* 2 vols. 1785. Reprint. New York: Garland, 1970.

Richetti, John J. *Popular Fiction Before Richardson: Narrative Patterns, 1700-1739.* Oxford: Clarendon Press, 1964.

Riley, E. C. *Cervantes' Theory of the Novel.* Oxford: Clarendon Press, 1962.

Sacks, Sheldon. *Fiction and the Shape of Belief: A Study of Henry Fielding with Glances at Swift, Johnson, and Richardson.* Berkeley: University of California Press, 1966.

Sandy, Gerald N. *Heliodorus.* Boston: Twayne, 1982.

Scarron, Paul. *The Comical Romance.* Edited by Benjamin Boyce. New York: Blom, 1968.

_____. *The Whole Comical Works of Monsr. Scarron.* Translated by Thomas Brown. 2 vols. 1700. Reprint. New York: Garland, 1973.

Schevill, Rudolph. "Studies in Cervantes: *Persiles y Sigismunda.*" *Modern Philology.* 4 (1906): 1-24, 667-704.

Schlauch, Margaret. *Antecedents of the English Novel: 1440-1600.* London: Oxford University Press, 1963.

Scholes, Robert, and Robert Kellogg. *The Nature of Narrative.* London: Oxford University Press, 1966.

Schulz, Dieter. " 'Novel,' 'Romance,' and Popular Fiction in the First Half of the Eighteenth Century." *Studies in Philology* 70 (1973), 77-91.

Scudéry, Georges de. "Preface to Ibrahim." Translated by Henry Cogan. In *Prefaces to Fiction.* Augustan Reprint Society, no. 32. 1952. Reprint. New York: Kraus Reprint, 1967.

Scudéry, Madeleine de. *Ibrahim, or the Illustrious Bassa.* Translated by Henry Cogan. London, 1674.

Sherbo, Arthur. *Studies in the Eighteenth Century Novel.* East Lansing: Michigan State University Press, 1969.

Sherburn, George. "Fielding's *Amelia:* An Interpretation," *English Literary History* 1 (1936): 1-14.

Showalter, English, Jr. *The Evolution of the French Novel: 1641-1782.* Princeton: Princeton University Press, 1972.

Smith, G. Gregory, ed. *Elizabethan Critical Essays.* 2 vols. London: Oxford University Press, 1904.

Sorel, Charles. *The Extravagant Shepherd.* Translated from the French. London, 1654.

Spilka, Mark. "Comic Resolution in Fielding's *Joseph Andrews.*" *College English* 15 (1953): 11-19.

Stegmann, Tilbert Diego. *Cervantes' Musterroman Persiles: Epentheorie and Romanpraxis um 1600.* Hamburg: Harmut, Lüdke Verlag, 1971.

Stevick, Philip. "Fielding and the Meaning of History." *PMLA* 79 (1964): 561-68.

Thornbury, Ethel M. *Henry Fielding's Theory of the Comic Prose Epic.* 1931. Reprint. New York: Russell, 1966.

Tillyard, E. M. W. *The English Epic and Its Background.* 1954. Reprint. New York: Oxford University Press, 1966.

————. *The Epic Strain in the English Novel.* London: Chatto and Windus, 1963.

Warren, F. M. *A History of the Novel Previous to the Seventeenth Century.* New York: Henry Holt, 1895.

Watt, Ian. *The Rise of the Novel: Studies in Defoe, Richardson, and Fielding.* Berkeley: University of California Press, 1964.

Weinbrot, Howard D. "Chastity and Interpolation: Two Aspects of *Joseph Andrews.*" *JEGP* 69 (1970): 14-31.

Williams, Ioan. *The Idea of the Novel in Europe: 1600-1800.* New York: New York University Press, 1979.

Wolff, Samuel Lee. *The Greek Romances in Elizabethan Prose Fiction.* New York: Columbia University Press, 1912.

Wright, Andrew. *Henry Fielding: Mask and Feast.* Berkeley: University of California Press, 1966.

Zimic, Stanislav. "El *Persiles* como Crítica de las Novela Bizantina." *Acta Neophilologica* 3 (1970): 49-64.

Index